Organizing for Generative AI and the Productivity Revolution

Reshaping Organizational Roles in the Age of Artificial Intelligence

Arthur J. O'Connor

Apress®

Organizing for Generative AI and the Productivity Revolution: Reshaping Organizational Roles in the Age of Artificial Intelligence

Arthur J. O'Connor
New York, NY, USA

ISBN-13 (pbk): 979-8-8688-0958-3   ISBN-13 (electronic): 979-8-8688-0959-0
https://doi.org/10.1007/979-8-8688-0959-0

Managing Director, Apress Media LLC: Welmoed Spahr
Acquisitions Editor: Shivangi Ramachandran
Development Editor: James Markham
Project Manager: Jessica Vakili

Cover designed by eStudioCalamar

Distributed to the book trade worldwide by Apress Media, LLC, 1 New York Plaza, New York, NY 10004, U.S.A. Phone 1-800-SPRINGER, fax (201) 348-4505, e-mail orders-ny@springer-sbm.com, or visit www.springeronline.com. Apress Media, LLC is a California LLC and the sole member (owner) is Springer Science + Business Media Finance Inc (SSBM Finance Inc). SSBM Finance Inc is a **Delaware** corporation.

For information on translations, please e-mail booktranslations@springernature.com; for reprint, paperback, or audio rights, please e-mail bookpermissions@springernature.com.

Apress titles may be purchased in bulk for academic, corporate, or promotional use. eBook versions and licenses are also available for most titles. For more information, reference our Print and eBook Bulk Sales web page at http://www.apress.com/bulk-sales.

Any source code or other supplementary material referenced by the author in this book is available to readers on GitHub (https://github.com/Apress). For more detailed information, please visit https://www.apress.com/gp/services/source-code.

If disposing of this product, please recycle the paper

To Linda: my guiding light, my North Star

Table of Contents

About the Author

Arthur J. O'Connor is the head of the MS in Data Science and BS in Information Systems degree programs at the City University of New York. He has over 20 years of experience as a senior corporate executive and IT management consultant. A graduate of the Newhouse School of Journalism at Syracuse University, he earned his MBA in finance from Fordham University and his Doctorate of Professional Studies from the Lubin School of Business at Pace University.

About the Technical Reviewer

 **Sam Adhikari** is the Generative AI-Powered SaaS Product Head at Sysoft Corporation. He has 30+ years of experience in AI, data science, and business intelligence. He leads development, support, and marketing of AI-powered supply chain management, eProcurement, contract management, spend analytics, supplier relationship management, optimization, logistics, financial reporting, and risk management of Software as a Service (SaaS) products. He earned a master's degree in AI and data science from Stanford University. He also earned additional master's degrees in Bioengineering and Aerospace Engineering from Temple University and City University of NY. He served as the chair of Software Technical Committee and Aerospace Cybersecurity Working Group at the American Institute of Aeronautics and Astronautics (AIAA). He is a Certified Information Systems Auditor (CISA) and Certified Data Privacy Solutions Engineer (CDPSE).

Introduction

"If at first you don't succeed, then skydiving definitely isn't for you."

—Steven Wright, comedian

So here's the thing.

If you're like most execs, you're being inundated with information overload about the productivity or cognitive revolution or Industry 4.0 and how Generative AI is going to change the nature of work, especially for knowledge workers.

You've read about the dawn of artificial general intelligence (AGI), or when machines become sentient, or the Singularity (roughly defined when machine intelligence exceeds human intelligence) – and how it's already here, only a matter of time, not until 30 years away, or probably never going to happen.

You sometimes get the sense that at least some of the "experts" who are evangelizing about all this stuff don't really know what they're talking about – that they're posing as techies but have probably never written a line of code in their lives.

You hear the term "Gen AI FOMO" a lot more often than you'd like – particularly from your business heads. "The new tech arms race" gets bandied about as well. A board member or two may have even called you after watching a news segment on how AI is going to make the primary business of the company obsolete.

The Self-perpetuating Hype Cycle

One needs to bear in mind – a phenomenon that doesn't get much airplay – that the same people who are writing and researching Gen AI are getting exposed to increasing amount of stories about Gen AI, due to the machine learning algorithms that serve up user-tailored content based on their keyword search history and page views.

As a result, the very people who are writing about the adoption of Gen AI are getting conditioned to believe from what they see and read that just about everyone else is also talking about and using Gen AI.

Fear Factor

And let's face it; it is kind of scary when you think about it. We're talking about machines that don't just crunch numbers but create wholly original content from repositories of the near entirety of all human knowledge, called foundation models, using artificial neural networks running in massive arrays in gigantic server farms to regurgitate, recombine, and synthesize insights and expertise in new and surprisingly effective ways.[1]

More recently are developments in autonomous, intelligent agents that can master sophisticated tasks in complex environments and vast strategy spaces, continually learning and iteratively adjusting their actions. Emerging from that field of AI research is an area of intelligent agent reinforcement learning called "self-play," whereby agents make copies of themselves and compete against each other, so that the training datasets

---

[1] In a test of 32 traits of empathy and judgment, Google's AMIE (Articulate Medical Intelligence Explorer), an LLM specialized for doctor/patient interactions, outperformed 20 primary care doctors on 28 out of 32 characteristics and tied on the other four. Tu, T., Palepu, A., Schaekermann, M., Saab, K., Freyberg, J., Tanno, R., Wang, A., Li, B., Amin, M., Tomasev, N. and Azizi, S., 2024. Towards conversational diagnostic AI. arXiv preprint arXiv:2401.05654.

from their interactions are no longer limited to human creativity or knowledge.[2] This creates the potential for models to develop and execute strategies beyond the capacity of human experience and intelligence.

Yikes!

All this while, vendors and consultants, large and small, are pitching you left and right, and the buzzwords are flying like an avalanche moving down a mountain. There are now literally hundreds of thousands of open source foundation (and mixture of expert and multi-modal) models that are being refined and fine-tuned for increasingly specialized domains and downstream tasks/use cases.[3] And closed-source model providers are expanding their platforms and specialized/customized service offerings every day, offering users to mess with their proprietary tensor weights and parameters to create their own variations of pre-trained large language models (LLMs) – for a (often substantial) price.

And with LLM's performance increases doubling about every 8 months – faster than computer chips as per Moore's Law[4] – you're left wondering what to do.

If this all sounds familiar, then this book is for you.

Wally World

You've probably noticed recently that your head of IT has stopped obsessing about "the cloud" (which is the good news) but now keeps talking about the risks of "Shadow AI" – better known back in the day as "End User

---

[2] Self-play: A classic technique to train competitive agents in adversarial games, Huggingface, https://huggingface.co/learn/deep-rl-course/en/unit7/self-play

[3] There are currently over 300,000 LLM variants listed on Hugging Face: https://huggingface.co/

[4] Ho, Anson, Tamay Besiroglu, Ege Erdil, David Owen, Robi Rahman, Zifan Carl Guo, David Atkinson, Neil Thompson, and Jaime Sevilla. "Algorithmic progress in language models." arXiv preprint arXiv:2403.05812 (2024)

Computing." The term refers to the development and production of IT technology outside the safeguards of IT departments and their associated controls, standards, and policies – exposing the organization to all kinds of strange, dangerous, and nasty ethical, reputational, and legal risks such as copyright infringement lawsuits – and, inversely, the unintentional leakage of internal proprietary intellectual property by those enthusiastic souls who strive making the output from their prompts more relevant by interrogating LLM's with company-specific (confidential) information.

Your head of IT is not wrong. That's both the good news and bad news about the **democratization of expertise** and dangers of the separation of **knowledge** from **understanding**. There are no regulatory guidelines or industry standards for AI; no consistent, universally accepted ground rules to go by (as yet). With Gen AI, anyone can create stuff, and organizations are struggling to develop policies to ban or proscribe the proper use of these tools.[5]

It's Wally World – the Wild, Wild West. And these things are nearly everywhere you look.

As you walk the corridors of your office, you see employees using chatbots to draft emails, memos, reports, and presentations. Software developers are using code bots to generate and test computer code, which are getting better and better at writing and reviewing programs. And if you're one of those organizations that still have writers, editors, illustrators, and/or graphic designers on staff, you can see they're hunched over the keyboards examining their prompts (aka prompt engineering), experimenting with ways to frame questions to get better results.

You may have already used some features to summarize lengthy/back-and-forth email threads or videos without having to watch them, take minutes for video meetings without having to attend them, or create presentations with animations and/or striking visuals that would otherwise require hours of work with the graphics.

---

[5] https://www.cnn.com/2023/09/22/tech/generative-ai-corporate-policy/index.html

Maybe you've used a chatbot to improve your writing by pasting your draft and asking it to tailor your message to a particular audience or address more clearly a certain issue or concern. Or ask it to make your point of view stronger by supplying examples or more dramatic hypothetical scenarios. Or summarize a stack of reports and draft the collective analysis/synthesis/digest of all of them. Or uploaded a pitch deck, asking the LLM for CEO-level-perspective feedback on approach and strategy.

Perhaps you've decided to be even more ambitious and used an LLM to create a vendor contract or full proposal, with business requirements, use cases, data models, financials, and functional specifications. All you needed to do was to upload the requirements for the RFP (request for proposal) and then ask for specific, point-by-point responses, based on your firm's solution delivery methodology.

Easy peasy.

And in most cases, this is all perfectly legit, provided that you know better than to avoid divulging confidential or proprietary information in your prompts or asking for details that the LLM probably doesn't know (they tend to be good at general information, not so much with specifics or calculations) and that of course you always check and validate output for factual accuracy, as these models can lie so consistently and convincingly.

Yes, a Fundamental Change Is Afoot

Experiencing this sudden, widespread user adoption firsthand,[6] you get the sense that some fundamental change is afoot: the automation of knowledge work. And of course, everyone's heard this one:

---

[6] According to OpenAI, ChatGPT acquired 1 million users just 5 days after launching in November 2022.

Generative AI won't replace you; but people using it will.[7]

And that threat sounds entirely feasible, especially for people whose jobs exclusively focus on creating, summarizing, and translating text or visual content, or in other cases, writing or testing (relatively simple and/or short snippets of) software code – what the current state of generative AI offerings do best.

As the research firm McKinsey notes:

> *"Although generative AI is still in the early stages, the potential applications for businesses are significant and wide-ranging. Generative AI can be used to write code, design products, create marketing content and strategies, streamline operations, analyze legal documents, provide customer service via chat bots, and even accelerate scientific discovery."*[8]

The potential and promise of Gen AI is that solution development will no longer be the purview of specialists or experts following a detailed, tedious, time-consuming methodology – but instead be done by anyone, almost instantaneously – with results limited only by users' creativity and imagination.

Call it the democratization of competency, systems that magically close the gap between novices and experts.[9] And their potential impact on productivity is hard to miss: instead of requiring a team of business analysts to produce business and functional requirements, developers

---

[7] Attributed to Economist Richard Baldwin, at the 2023 World Economic Forum's Growth Summit.

[8] "Generative AI and the future of work in America," McKinsey Center for Government July 2023 p. 4

[9] Use of Gen AI enhances the performance of novices more than experts. Inkpen, Kori & Chappidi, Shreya & Mallari, Keri & Nushi, Besmira & Ramesh, Divya & Michelucci, Pietro & Mandava, Vani & Vepřek, Libuše & Quinn, Gabrielle. (2023). Advancing Human-AI Complementarity: The Impact of User Expertise and Algorithmic Tuning on Joint Decision Making. ACM Transactions on Computer-Human Interaction. 30. 10.1145/3534561.

to generate and review code, and system engineering and QA teams to conduct performance, security, and (unit, system, and user acceptance) testing, anyone can write a prompt to a code bot that will generate and run the code.

To quote a recent Harvard Business Review working paper, "We suggest that the capabilities of AI create a 'jagged technological frontier' where some tasks are easily done by AI, while others, though seemingly similar in difficulty level, are outside the current capability of AI."[10]

In other words, it's not just about whether, or to what degree, you use Gen AI; it's knowing how to use it and for what types of tasks (understanding what it currently does well and not so well). After all, there's a lot to learn about interrogating and fine-tuning LLMs. And, as they say, "Basic prompts result in boring output."

And much of the literature frames the key management challenge as finding the right use cases that demonstrate value: the low-hanging fruit, the quick wins, so-called "tactical implementations" of "lean AI" mostly involving small (not large) language models.

This book argues that it's not just about finding the right fit-for-purpose use cases. It's also about organizational readiness and capability.

And that's the real danger of the hype: enamored by the palpably stunning technology, many executives and decision-makers are overestimating their internal capacity to effectively make use of these tools. Cold, hard realism about internal organizational talent and ability is being replaced by wishful thinking, often engendered by the song and dance of enthusiastic vendors.

And you know how that story ends...

---

[10] Dell'Acqua, Fabrizio, Edward McFowland III, Ethan Mollick, Hila Lifshitz-Assaf, Katherine C. Kellogg, Saran Rajendran, Lisa Krayer, François Candelon, and Karim R. Lakhani. "Navigating the Jagged Technological Frontier: Field Experimental Evidence of the Effects of AI on Knowledge Worker Productivity and Quality." Harvard Business School Working Paper, No. 24-013, September 2023

But What Is It Really Good For?

Now the counter argument to all this hype comes from those who get the nagging feeling that all of this fanfare amounts to advances in technology in search of a practical use. Big tech firms are spending gazillions of dollars building massive, more powerful models, but the market is still figuring out what to do with them.

In the lingo of Silicon Valley, there's no clear "killer app" for Gen AI, defined as a feature, function, or application that makes it indispensable or indisputably superior to other products.

At least not yet.

And, as history has shown, what is suddenly made technologically possible (in the case of Gen AI, dramatic reductions in processing cost/performance of server farms, along with amazing advances in artificial neural network architectures) isn't always terribly useful, beneficial, or even desired.

As author and software engineer Molly White put it: "You can't build a hundred-billion-dollar industry around a technology that's kind of useful, mostly in mundane ways, and that boasts perhaps small increases in productivity if and only if the people who use it fully understand its limitations."[11]

And these critics have a point: aside from performing some pretty neat tricks, the current generation of models don't appear to be revolutionary, game changers, or industry disruptors.

But perhaps the operative word in that last sentence is "current" (as in current generation). Perhaps it's wise for leaders to focus not so much on what these systems can do now, but what they appear to be capable of doing soon.

---

[11] "AI ain't useless. But is it worth it?" https://www.citationneeded.news/ai-isnt-useless/

Learning Curve

Some of this lack of deeper user adoption can be attributed to lack of unfamiliarity of what AI tools are capable of doing - we're just starting to move up the learning curve.

Many people seem to be using these tools as supercharged chatbots – and they are great (but not perfect) at retrieving the information and generating a relevant answer to a query. But their real power lies in their "intelligence" – from their training on massive bodies of knowledge to (mathematically) understand associations, constructs, and insights.

For example, when starting a research project, instead of prompting the LLM for sources on the topic, perhaps a better prompt would be to ask advice on how best to go about conducting the project: what useful insights or factors should be considered, based on what previous researchers and experts have done.

You can ask AI to interview you in order to give it more context and understanding of the nature and scope of work. These tools can serve as your own personal adviser, mentor, planner, colleague, coach, and tutor – not merely as a chatbot or search engine.

Purpose of This Book

While there are many works that go into the profound structural social and economic changes that Gen AI may bring to how we all work and live – the power of deep fakes to deceive and spread disinformation, the growing sophistication of cybersecurity threats, and the rise of a host of social and ethical issues, notably data privacy and the widening of the digital divide – this book focuses on the impact of Industry 4.0 on organizational behavior, with an emphasis on describing the new types of roles and competencies that are required to successfully harness the power of this new generation of technology.

Ultimately, this book is a leadership guide, a handbook to help executives build the right capabilities with the right teams to succeed.

The book is designed to help executives, managers, and other decision-makers understand the significant changes in organizational roles and responsibilities that these current and emerging technologies require, focusing on the expanded roles of the Data Scientist, Software Engineer, Data Engineer, Data Analyst, DevOps, Model Risk Manager/ Auditor, Machine Learning Architect, and ML Product Manager – functions responsible for the development, design, production, implementation, monitoring, maintenance, retraining, and governance of these models.

Why the focus on these roles? Because understanding how these AI systems work requires a basic competency in Data Science. It's entirely possible that AI may supplant or replace the field of Data Science in the next few years, as specialized code repos and code bots proliferate and evolve, essentially automating the tasks and workflows of Data Scientists and Data Engineers.

The book's thesis in a nutshell: these new types of tools and processes require a radically different set of functions and type of competency model from the traditional and typical Ops and Tech organization. Just as there are all kinds of important new things to learn and understand about the nature, design, and use of large language models and generative AI, there are also critical implications of these same phenomena to the structure and behaviors of most large organizations.

Moving Fast, Safely

To be clear, the book does NOT propose that organizations move slowly and cautiously before adopting Gen AI, as that is a recipe for competitive disadvantage. This book is for the organizational leader who wants to embrace some of these game-changing technologies – but who insists on developing the requisite **organizational capabilities** to ensure successful implementation.

How do organizations move fast safely? To draw an analogy: the same way race car teams ensure the safety of their drivers. It's not by telling them to drive slowly and carefully. To keep drivers safe, they modify cars with structural features and additional safety equipment; drivers are outfitted with fire-resistant suits and safety helmets.

The organizational capabilities described in this book are like those roll cages and safety harnesses – functional features that enable organizations to move fast to design and implement Gen AI systems, safely, effectively, and successfully.

Key Takeaway Message

The one big takeaway message of this book is this: that for most organizations, successful adoption of Gen AI largely comes down to **selecting** (or subscribing to) the right foundational model(s) – or mixture of expert models – and **adapting** it/them to reengineer and create new capabilities and processes, with the right control processes and safeguard in place, at the right cost relative to expected return, to ensure a sufficient return on capital, as the computing cost of training new foundation models is beyond the resources of most organizations. According to Stanford's AI Index estimates, the training costs of OpenAI's GPT-4 required $78 million worth of compute to train, while Google's Gemini Ultra cost $191 million.)[12]

---

[12] Nestor Maslej, Loredana Fattorini, Raymond Perrault, Vanessa Parli, Anka Reuel, Erik Brynjolfsson, John Etchemendy, Katrina Ligett, Terah Lyons, James Manyika, Juan Carlos Niebles, Yoav Shoham, Russell Wald, and Jack Clark, "The AI Index 2024 Annual Report," AI Index Steering Committee, Institute for Human-Centered AI, Stanford University, Stanford, CA, April 2024

That is, the trick is in understanding the trade-offs in cost, complexity, and variability – and perhaps most importantly – domain-specific training alignment with specific strategies and use cases, relative to costs, opportunities, risks, and deployment methods.

To boil all down to three guiding principles:

1. There's literally no way you can keep up with the major advances and new developments in Intelligent Systems. Instead, concentrate on building strong teams with the right mandates and robust development processes to ensure that the solutions fit your business strategies and use cases while ensuring the data are of high quality, the risks managed, the outcomes tested, and the results measured and validated.

2. Above all be flexible; don't be intimidated or bullied by the technocrats into believing there's only one way of doing things.

3. And never forget that, while there's a great deal of new things to come, there are some age-old axioms that remain: keep your people, processes, and systems focused on serving your customers (after all, they pay the bills), but don't forget the needs and concerns of all of your stakeholders.

Major Obstacle: Organizational Capabilities Mismatch

There are, however, major obstacles in pursuing this strategy: if your organization is structured and staffed like most businesses, you most likely do not have the organizational **functions** and **capabilities** (power hierarchies, skills sets, personality types, roles and responsibilities) in place to pull this off.

And you're not alone. Most organizations – especially corporate IT departments, designed for the previous Digital Revolution, – are not currently structured, staffed, and organizationally aligned and behaviorally incentivized to effectively implement Gen AI in mission-critical processes.

And, as you might imagine, that fact alone creates all kinds of problems for you, the organizational leader.

By this realignment, we don't mean a reduction or expansion of the standard corporate IT organization (management, procurement, security, network administration, systems analysis and architecture, service and support desks). We mean different **types** of **capabilities**, requiring different job functions, skills sets, roles, responsibilities, incentives, and reporting structures.

So in order to achieve that goal, the current IT organization – currently staffed by technocrats hired for their ability to manage the care and feeding of an increasingly complex, heterogeneous computing environment (both on premises and/or in the cloud) – needs to be transformed.

Emerging Organizational Model in the Age of Intelligent Systems

While the main focus of this book is not about new/emerging organizational structures (again, it's about all the new functions, roles, skill sets, and personas that come with adopting Gen AI), it would be remiss not to at least theorize on what the new organizational model will look like in the next few years.

This new model is evolving, but it will most likely represent a major change to the traditional corporate IT organization. After all, the mission will no longer be about managing development teams to suss out business requirements from users and translate them into functional specifications, as well as production teams to source and support sufficient, secure, and reliable computing and communication environments to enable business processes.

Instead, we envision the new mission and target operating model will be primarily about **empowerment**, where nearly every employee is a designer, developer, and tester. The primary mission of the Chief AI Officer (CAIO) and staff will be to ensure the security, performance, integrity, and systems support of the overriding architecture/AI ecosystem across the enterprise.

What will the new type of IT organization look like? The model might look a bit like a combination of think tank, research lab, venture capital firm, and incubator, staffed with talent scouts, deal-makers, diplomats, security experts, and technocrats to keep abreast of the many different types of available tools and platforms to create and enable better and disruptive business strategies. [Yes, we're pretty sure technocrats will still be needed in cross-functional and matrixed management roles, if for no other reason than to keep the traditional organizational silos and staff functions running – good news for all us technocrats.]

Structure of This Book

As noted, the mission of this book is to help you, the executive, understand the change in functions and organizational capabilities that are required to successfully implement and embed AI models in core business processes.

In the first three chapters (Part I) of this book, we'll consider a short history of previous industrial revolutions – how we got to where we are today. We'll also talk about how IT organizations have embraced "ML Ops" as an outgrowth of DevOps, as the first evolutionary stage in implementing machine learning models in mission-critical processes. That's all in Chapter 1.

In Chapter 2, we'll review an old topic but one that takes on even greater significance in the age of Gen AI, Data Governance, and the new data management challenges involved.

As you will see (and one of the key messages of this book), Data Governance is a prerequisite capability because the application of Gen AI for most organizations isn't about creating LLMs but customizing them for specific use cases using internal and external data sources (datasets not included in the training data of the LLMs) via techniques such as Retrieval Augmented Generation (RAG). Only when internal and often proprietary data sources are discoverable and validated, they can be used with integration frameworks such as LangChain to connect with open source and/or closed-source third-party models and to orchestrate the sequence of functions across different language models.

In the following chapter (Chapter 3), we cover Corporate Governance, outlining the many changes in organizational roles and functions required to effectively harness the power of these AI models.

In Part II, we discuss the current and future state of Gen AI adoption and the future of leadership in the intelligent machines.

In Part III, we discuss how law-makers and regulators are shaping regulatory compliance requirements and what academic researchers are discovering about the impact of Gen AI in the workplace. The final chapter serves as the book's conclusion.

PART I

Yesterday, Today, and Tomorrow

CHAPTER 1

The History and Potential Future of Human–Machine Collaboration

"To lead in times like this will require the eyes of an artist who sees the broad shape of things, not an analyst who sees data points."

—Peggy Noonan, political columnist

With the emergence of Gen AI, academic researchers have begun to explore the impact of AI technologies on organizational leadership, particularly in the areas of automation, engagement, decision-making, and innovation, which could change traditional corporate power hierarchies and organizational structures.[1] As a professor at the University College London put it in his article in Columbia Business Law Review,

---

[1] Benbya, Hind & Pachidi, Stella & Jarvenpaa, Sirkka. (2021). Artificial Intelligence in Organizations: Implications for Information Systems Research. Journal of the Association for Information Systems. 22. 10.17705/1jais.00662

© Arthur J. O'Connor 2024
A. J. O'Connor, *Organizing for Generative AI and the Productivity Revolution*,
https://doi.org/10.1007/979-8-8688-0959-0_1

recent developments "...clearly highlight AI's growing importance in management and hint at the enormous changes that corporate leadership may experience in the future."[2]

In this chapter, we take a step back to consider the organizational effects of past industrial revolutions, share some more thoughts about the impact of Gen AI on current roles and functions, and discuss some future organizational implications that the AI revolution may bring.

Deja Vu

Chances are there's something familiar about all this talk of organizational transformation in order to adapt to new technology. You've seen this movie before.

Some of the hype about AI is reminiscent of that phase when your company embarked on a bold initiative called Data Warehousing and/or real-time Business Intelligence in the 1990s and the 2000s.

In this new paradigm, the company was to become a "data-driven business," where all of the information from all over the organization was to be (virtually) centralized, so that anyone anywhere could just pull up a dashboard to see what was going on (which probably struck you as a bit odd at the time, as it had been your experience in the Corporate World that data are mostly used by management to justify – not make – key decisions).

And as we all know by now, things didn't quite work out that way.

Departments kept creating and building their own data stores, with their own dashboard and reports on the metrics that they cared most about (a.k.a., "data feudalism"). They tend to develop their own data systems because internal IT organizations "move too slowly." That's because corporate IT departments have to abide by software development

---

[2] Petrin, M. (2019). Corporate Management in the Age of AI. Columbia Business Law Review, 2019(3), 965–1030. https://doi.org/10.7916/cblr.v2019i3.5118

methodologies, IT governance processes, controls, and technical standards and an information security bureaucracy that plain old business units can bypass (at least until Internal Audit finds out about it).

Hence the data silos and "knowledge fiefdoms" that still exist today and continue to flourish.

Why This Time Might Be Different

But this time – given the scope and power of this new technology wave – it may be different.

Just consider how the most recent previous industrial revolution, the Digital Revolution, changed the nature of work for most people.

Some 50 years ago if you walked into the facilities of a large organization, you could make a good guess at what type of business it was in; there were different types of equipment, different stores of raw materials and supplies, with different types of floor plan layouts.

In today's Information Age, you notice that just about all offices look the same: people sitting in rows of cubicles hunched over their desktop computers keying in data, mostly likely sending or responding to emails.

Historically, organizational roles and hierarchical power structures have been slowest to adapt to technological change, so it's no surprise that most organizations find themselves "behind the curve" in the face of new, transformational change. The phenomenon is known as "organizational inertia."[3]

---

[3] Kelly, Dawn, and Terry L. Amburgey. "Organizational inertia and momentum: A dynamic model of strategic change." Academy of management journal 34, no. 3 (1991): 591-612

A Very Short Historical Perspective

In some sense, the new Productivity Revolution can be seen as the next evolutionary stage of previous industrial revolutions.

For some (very short) historical perspective, let's consider the impacts to the workplace from the initial Industrial Revolution. The seminal works of two men immediately come to mind.

At the rise of the machine age, a Scottish economist and philosopher named Adam Smith (1723–1790) published in 1776, "An Inquiry into the Nature and Causes of the Wealth of Nations," which argued for the division of labor in the workplace that made possible significant improvements in process efficiency.

A century later, a mechanical engineer named Frederick Taylor (1856–1915) observed that the introduction of machines in the workplace made possible incredible breakthroughs in process efficiency and output if work was designed and monitored to maximize output.

The rest, as they say, was economic history: the rise of division of labor and explosion in worker productivity, which led to dramatic increases in economic growth and improvements in the standard of living. For years, worker productivity rose hand-in-hand with worker income. As output per worker increased, so did the wages earned.

Until it didn't, starting in about 1979, when something strange happened (Figure 1-1).[4]

In scientific circles, the phenomenon is called "Punctuated Equilibrium."[5] Translation: "things don't really change that much over time – until they suddenly do." That year, productivity in the United States began to grow faster than income – in fact over four times faster, from 1979 to 2022, as shown in Figure 1-1.

---

[4] "The Productivity–Pay Gap," Economic Policy Institute, https://www.epi.org/productivity-pay-gap/

[5] https://en.wikipedia.org/wiki/Punctuated_equilibrium

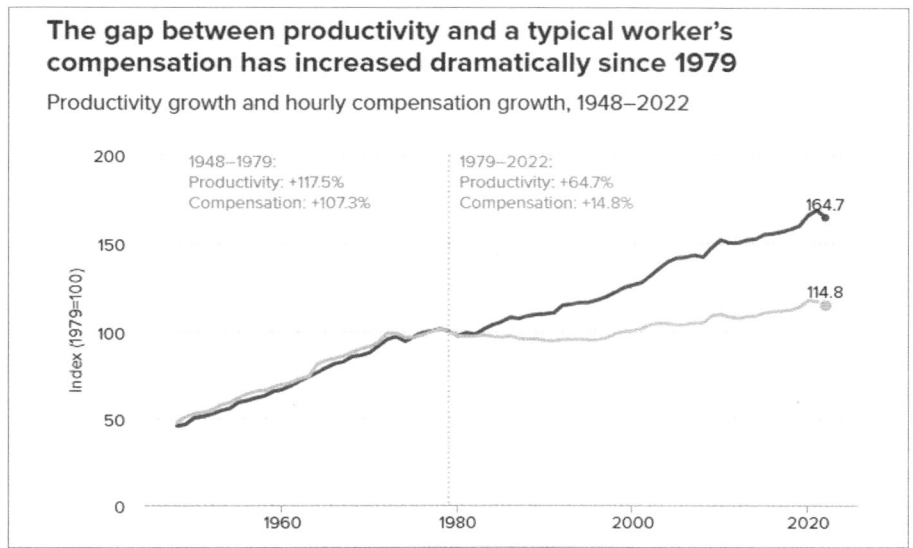

Figure 1-1. *The relationship of productivity growth and hourly compensation growth, 1948–2022*[6]

There's no conclusive, widely accepted explanation among economists as to the cause of this seismic rift, but an entirely plausible explanation has to do with the advent of the Digital Revolution, which coincided with the proliferation of computers, smart phones, and all sorts of digital gadgets we have today.

In other words, the previous Digital Revolution may well have set the stage for the generative AI Revolution, in which capital, in the form of Intellectual Property as well as monetary and fixed assets, is supplanting human workers as the primary sources for creating economic growth.

---

[6] "The Productivity Pay Gap," Economic Policy Institute, updated Oct 2022. https://www.epi.org/productivity-pay-gap/#:~:text=The%20result%20 of%20this%20policy, (after%20adjusting%20for%20inflation)

What types of changes are we talking about? The easiest example to cite is the role of any content creator. Nearly all types (designers, bloggers, authors, podcasters, software coders, copywriters, researchers, and illustrators) need to become (a much smaller group of) prompt engineers and become well-versed in privacy, copyright, and responsible AI compliance standards.

As we've noted in the Introduction, the biggest change may be to the traditional corporate IT organization: transitioning their mission, skills sets, and reporting structures from the care, feeding, and growth of the computing infrastructure to something resembling a multi-disciplinary task force focused on empowering others to develop and enable new business models, products, services, processes – made possible through new generations of cloud-based AI systems, by which real-time (or near real-time) external data (Retrieval Augmented Generation) is integrated with internal proprietary data in an LLM (via fine-tuning and embeddings in vector databases) to create insights into market opportunities and competitive challenges.

Changes Already Taking Place

Here are some key areas where broad scale adoption of these tools is already happening:

- Development and Coding: Developers are switching from manual coding to using software development environments like Cognition Labs' Devin AI for code generation.[7]

---

[7] Note that, at some point, when code doesn't need to be maintained by humans, many of the concerns and requirements of code reviewers – clarity and adequacy of documentation, how well the code is structured, reusability, modularity, need for abstraction boundaries –may not be a concern!

- IT Support: Teams are using AI-powered chatbots for handling routine tasks and maintaining a human touch for more complex issues.

- Cybersecurity: Professionals are using AI tools for threat detection, continuous training on emerging threats, continuous automated internal audits using penetration testing tools and other detection and prevention controls, and maintaining a balance between human intuition and AI-driven analysis.

And it's not just roles and functions that are starting to change. There are changes in organizational structures now emerging to help organizations best harness the productivity potential of these pattern-matching, intelligent mega-machines.

But before we get into that, perhaps it's worth it to give a bit of background in the Software Development Lifecycle (SDLC).

The Software Development Lifecycle

Like everything, software has a lifecycle: a business need results in code being written, maintained, and eventually the software is replaced. Software development is an integrated and automated process, with mature tools that check, test, and even deploy software automatically.

Software is a team sport usually written by multiple developers requiring specialization in software components. Developers focus on the areas such as networking, the user interface, servers, and business logic. Operations teams were responsible for supporting software in production, and to make sure that there was no gap between development and operations, they are usually combined into a single team: DevOps (we'll go into this term a bit later).

Bottom line is this: software is far too large and complex to be written by a single person. But it wasn't always like this.

For some historical perspective: the process of writing and updating code has radically changed over the last 30 years. Initially, there were few automation tools to make a developer's life easier. A developer typically saved code on a local drive, and if it failed later in a system or user acceptance testing phase, it was up to that developer to manually fix the integration issues.

The tools were not reliable, and there were few standards. It was easier for a developer to write their own program and then figure out how it worked with other applications. Integration was an after-thought, and proficient developers were scarce, requiring them to be involved in the entire process including testing and deploying to production. And yes, even getting up at 3:00 AM to provide support if there was a system failure.

If there was a dedicated operations team, they were a separate team and didn't have the expertise or knowledge to identify the issue. The developer was still woken up at 3 in the morning.

Not surprising, problems arose. Just look at what happened at Knight Capital, back in 2012.[8]

Case Study: Knight Capital

At 9:30 AM on August 1, 2012, the automated trading systems at Knight Capital began executing trades for their customers when the market opened. The company had existed for almost 20 years and was a major player in automated trading of stocks on the NASDAQ stock exchange. The Knight trading software system, SMARS, had been a proven system utilized for over 10 years. Within 45 minutes, SMARS had purchased $3.5 billion of stocks via millions of orders, resulting in 4 million executions in 154 stocks for more than 397 million shares.

---

[8] Security and Exchange Commission Administrative Proceedings, File No. 3-15570: https://www.sec.gov/files/litigation/admin/2013/34-70694.pdf

At 9:45 AM, Knight CEO Thomas Joyce was informed that Knight Capital had lost over $400 million and, within a day, it ceased to exist as a company and he resigned. What could have caused this? There was a bug in the SMARS code rolled out the night before, exacerbated by the fact that only 7 of the 8 systems were upgraded.

In essence, the company was destroyed by simple human error: a careless technician who manually copied new software to SMARS, as part of a routine upgrade done hundreds of times before. The incident highlighted the importance of automated rigorous and managed processes for software development.

A more recent example was that one bad configuration update of Crowdstrike's Falcon sensor antivirus software to Microsoft Windows in July 2024 that resulted in thousands of airline flights cancellations delays in public transit systems in major cities, disruptions in appointments at hospitals and healthcare clinics, as well as payments suspended in online banking systems and financial institutions around the world.[9]

The Rise of "ML Ops"

Much like the early days of software development, the process of data transformation and model training is very manual, requiring scarce talent. While the space is rapidly evolving, the tools are relatively immature, and thus much of the process is manual.

---

[9] "CrowdStrike outage explained: What caused it and what's next," Sean Michael Kerner, TechTarget, July 23, 2024 https://www.techtarget.com/whatis/feature/Explaining-the-largest-IT-outage-in-history-and-whats-next#:~:text=The%20root%20cause%20of%20the,on%20the%20Microsoft%20Windows%20OOS

While some parts can be automated, few tools work together end-to-end, resulting in a fragmented process. As a result, data scientists are involved in the entire process, from data gathering, model training, testing, production deployment, and even operations. The bane of many data scientists is that 3:00 AM call, as they are the only ones who may know why "the model is failing."

Machine learning is even more complex than software development, but the lack of tooling and complexity make it hard to collaborate. Sound familiar? AI has to go through a similar maturation process to what SDLC went through.

"ML Ops" is intended to resolve the profound difference in traditional software development lifecycle methodology (SDLC) and machine learning model development. "ML Ops" seeks to adopt best practices in Development Operations (DevOps) and Site Reliability Engineering (SRE) and apply them to model development processes.

To give some more background: the predecessor to "ML Ops" was DevOps, a management discipline to optimize the competing and conflicting interests between software development and production release management. Conflicts arose as developers are incentivized to push out great functionality faster, while site engineers are incentivized to ensure security, stability, and availability. The practice and organizational structure of DevOps seek to integrate, coordinate, and optimize the trade-offs from competing interests across these different IT functions.

"ML Ops" represents the next evolution, as machine learning models are inherently different from conventional software development.

Unlike nearly all traditional application development efforts, most machine learning and AI models never make it into production, due to their experimental nature. And because most models are never deployed, they don't need to undergo the rigors and control testing for performance, stability, and security that one would for a production environment release, as such measures are premature/unwarranted.

In this sense, the term "ML Ops" is a bit misleading, as model design and development is not primarily about the production release process, but really "...a set of standards, tools, processes and methodology that aims to minimize time wasted on abandoned, misguided or irrelevant work when solving a business problem or need"[10] (definition courtesy DataBricks).

The CAIO: All Hail, Explainer-in-Chief!

OK, that's great, you say. But who's going to lead this structural transformation of roles and functions?

In many large, global organizations, that role will fall to a new executive role, Chief Artificial Intelligence Officer (CAIO), responsible for the strategy and implementation of AI across the enterprise.

This leader, and attendant staff, will need to be part tech guru, evangelist, thought-leader, diplomat, solution architect, power broker, talent scout, deal-maker, and overlord - as well as risk assessor and mitigator, continuous internal auditor, and dashboard operator of Ai Ops KPIs.

But perhaps the most important role will be "Explainer-in-Chief," to provide the wisdom and guidance as to how best to acquire/develop, design, produce, monitor, maintain, and govern generative AI models.

This person will be supported by squadrons of interdisciplinary teams – composed of data scientists, software engineers, data engineers, data analysts, DevOp specialists, model risk managers, machine learning architects, and machine learning product managers. These roles, once relegated to behind-the-scenes back-office or decision-support staff functions, will evolve to become critical players in designing and deploying these new types of mission-critical systems.

---

[10] https://www.databricks.com/resources/ebook/the-big-book-of-mlops

As the number and variety of commercial specialized LLMs offerings expand, organizations will be able to harness their creative and analytical powers with faster and more cost-efficient development cycles.

And these new teams, as Explainers-in-Chief, are perhaps best suited to hash this all out for members of the C-suite, senior management teams, and board directors.

These roles will be tasked to build or buy and/or tailor the optimal large language model platform for harnessing creative and analytical powers with faster and more cost-efficient development cycles, along the following areas:

- Use Case Alignment: Identifying the specific use cases and applications where LLMs will be applied. Different platforms excel in different domains, so it's critical to choose the platform that aligns best with the organization's objectives.

- Model Capabilities: Evaluating the capabilities of the LLMs offered by each platform, considering factors such as natural language understanding, context retention, multilingual support, and the ability to handle specific tasks relevant to the organization.

- Training Data and Domain Expertise: Examining the availability and quality of training data for the domains relevant to the organization. Some platforms have pre-trained models tailored to specific industries or sectors, offering a head start in domain expertise.

- Customization and Fine-Tuning: Assessing the degree of customization and fine-tuning capabilities provided by each platform. The ability to adapt pre-trained models to specific organizational needs is crucial for achieving optimal performance.

- Integration with Existing Systems: Calibrating how well a LLM platform integrates with the existing systems and workflows. Seamless integration can streamline development cycles and enhance overall efficiency.

- Scalability and Performance: Evaluating the scalability of the LLM platform to ensure it can handle the expected workload; considering performance metrics, response times, and the platform's ability to scale as the organization's needs grow.

- Cost Structure: Understanding the pricing model of each LLM platform, based on subscription costs, usage-based pricing, and any additional fees; ensuring that the pricing aligns with the budget and has sufficient Return on Investment.

- Developer-Friendly Tools: Assessing the development environment and features provided by each platform, with sufficient documentation, API libraries, and support that can contribute to faster and more efficient development cycles.

- Ethical and Responsible AI Practices: Prioritizing platforms that adhere to ethical and responsible AI practices, based on factors such as bias mitigation, transparency, interpretability, and the platform's commitment to ethical considerations in AI development.

- Community and Support: Evaluating the community support and resources available for each LLM platform for valuable insights, support, and a collaborative environment for developers.

- Security and Compliance: Ensuring that the LLM platform adheres to security standards and compliance requirements relevant to the organization and industry.

- Updates and Maintenance: Considering the platform's approach to updates, bug fixes, and ongoing support contribute to long-term reliability.

The Frontier of Automation

We know what you're thinking; you've heard this all before. Maybe you've even heard talk of "post-labor economics" or "automated capitalism."

For now, we're not talking about the Singularity, Rise of the Machines, or the Robot Apocalypse. But for a book about the impact of generative AI on the nature of work and jobs, some points need to be raised.

Historically, the fear has always been that as automation increases, the demand for human workers decreases, which to date hasn't proved true. The Luddites were wrong. So far, industrial automation has spurred the growth of new types of jobs, often requiring higher cognitive skills for which humans perform better than machines.

But what happens when the cognitive capacity of machines starts to compete with or exceed that of most humans? That's never happened before in economic history.

The concept of the Frontier of Automation is useful here. It postulates that as the complexity of tasks that machines are capable of – both mechanical and cognitive – continues to advance (linearly, or in some opinions, exponentially), there will be less need for humans. As the task complexity/sphere of automation expands, eventually the frontier will encompass the entire sphere of human tasks. Some humans will stay ahead of the curve, but most won't. But human task complexity is seen as a bounded distribution, i.e., there's a limit to what people (even exceptionally gifted people) can do.

So will AI eventually supplant capitalism, and with it, our entire global economy? Will this new industrial revolution not just replace humans from low as well as higher level functions to the extent that new types of jobs **won't** be created, as they've always done in prior industrial revolutions?

Will the rise of AI restrict the need for human intervention, management, and oversight of such systems to only a small cadre of highly advanced specialists? Will our society fall into the hands of a few billionaire technocrats and their lackeys at a handful of enormous Big Tech firms that run the water- and power-hungry server farms?

And what about these "emergent behaviors" by large language models? What if these models, which have been trained on the corpus of human knowledge, start to transcend the cognitive capacity of humans and start to do things that humans can't even comprehend?

We don't know how this will all play out in the long run. The roles and functions of CAIO, CEO, CIO, CTO, and CDO may expand and perhaps supplant other executive roles. Organizational hierarchies may flatten; matrix structures could take over and even some silos could disappear.

Entire industries may well come to look more like Hollywood Studios; independent groups of creators pitch concepts, producers decide to fund (or not); directors and staff are recruited; project teams are assembled; the project goes into production and is released.

From what we've already seen, it sure looks like AI is going to upend the traditional white-collar knowledge worker, not unlike what industrial robots did for assembly line workers and computer numerical control (CNC) machines did to machinists.

What we **do** know for sure from studying this field and speaking with industry professionals is that the way most organizations are structured and operate – especially corporate IT departments – are woefully prepared and ill-suited for the age of Intelligent Machines, and thus need to adapt.

Redefining Leadership

In the brave new world of Gen AI, organizational leaders find themselves navigating uncharted waters, where the boundaries between human and machine grow ever more blurred.

At the heart of this conundrum lies a delicate balancing act: how to harness the boundless potential of Gen AI while preserving the essence of human ingenuity and creativity that has long been the lifeblood of their enterprises. After all, these artificial muses offer tantalizing promises – a wellspring of fresh ideas that could propel organizations to new heights, shattering long-held assumptions and upending traditional business models.

Perhaps the key lies in redefining the very nature of leadership itself. In this generative age, true leaders must become architects of collaboration, forging unlikely alliances between flesh and silicon, channeling the unique strengths of each to forge something greater than the sum of its parts. They must cultivate a spirit of experimentation, embracing the inevitable missteps and failures that accompany any bold endeavor.

Creating a Culture of Change, Curiosity, and Adaptability

In this sense, leadership is not a static state, but a constant evolution – a perpetual dance between human and machine, a delicate choreography of inspiration and iteration. Those who master this intricate pas de deux will emerge as the vanguards of a new era, ushering their organizations into realms of possibility hitherto unimagined.

To thrive in this new era, leaders must first cultivate a mindset of curiosity and adaptability. Gen AI represents a rapidly evolving force that will disrupt industries, business models, and ways of working. Leaders must be willing to challenge the status quo, embrace change, and foster a culture of continuous learning and experimentation, a holistic approach that spans people, processes, and technology.

First and foremost, as we reveal in the next chapter, leaders must recognize the pivotal role of data in fueling Gen AI models. Data is the lifeblood of these systems, and ensuring its quality, availability, and security is paramount. This requires a deep understanding of data governance, data pipelines, and data infrastructure. Leaders should empower their data scientists, data engineers, and data analysts to collaborate seamlessly, breaking down silos and fostering a data-driven culture.

As we go into detail in Part II of this book, leaders must equip their software engineers and operations teams with the tools and skills necessary to integrate Gen AI into existing systems and workflows. This may involve adopting new frameworks, architectures, and development methodologies that can seamlessly integrate with generative models. Continuous integration, deployment, and monitoring pipelines must be designed with generative AI in mind, ensuring scalability, reliability, and security.

As Gen AI systems become more prevalent, the role of model risk managers and auditors will take on new importance. These professionals will be responsible for ensuring that AI models are fair, ethical, and compliant with regulations. They will work closely with data scientists and machine learning architects to implement rigorous testing, validation, and monitoring processes, mitigating risks and ensuring transparency.

Machine learning architects will be the visionaries behind the organization's Gen AI strategies. They will design and engineer the overall AI system architectures, balancing the trade-offs between performance, scalability, and model complexity. These architects will need to stay abreast of the latest advancements in Gen AI, continuously exploring new techniques and approaches to push the boundaries of what's possible.

Bringing it all together, ML product managers will be the glue that binds the various teams and stakeholders involved in Gen AI initiatives. They will be responsible for translating business requirements into technical specifications, prioritizing feature roadmaps, and ensuring that Gen AI solutions deliver tangible value to customers and end users. Effective ML product managers will possess a unique blend of technical expertise, business acumen, and communication skills, bridging the gap between technology and business strategy.

To support this transformation, organizational leaders must invest in upskilling and reskilling their workforce. Continuous training and professional development programs should be established to ensure that employees stay up-to-date with the latest generative AI technologies, techniques, and best practices. Cross-functional collaboration and knowledge sharing should be encouraged, fostering a culture of innovation and collective intelligence.

Furthermore, leaders must become talent scouts by participating in the AI community and continuously surveying the scene to identify and attract top talent in the AI and data science domains, while ensuring to retain them by fostering a workplace culture that values creativity, intellectual curiosity, and a passion for pushing boundaries.

As businesses embrace Gen AI, leaders must also be mindful of the ethical and societal implications of these powerful technologies. They must establish clear ethical guidelines, ensuring that AI systems are developed and deployed in a responsible and transparent manner, free from bias and discrimination. Collaboration with academia, industry associations, and regulatory bodies will be crucial in navigating this complex landscape.

In the end, harnessing the power of Gen AI is not just about adopting new technologies; it's about reimagining the very essence of how businesses operate. Leaders who can strike the right balance between innovation, risk management, and ethical responsibility will be well-positioned to thrive in this new era of automated and enhanced business processes and disruptive business strategies.

Human–Machine Collaboration

So what will be the longer-term effects of the Productivity Resolution? As AI systems become more integrated into daily workflows, organizational structures will need to evolve to facilitate better collaboration between human workers and AI.

You might call it "Human-Machine Collaboration," as successful organizations recognize the need for a harmonious interaction between automated systems and human workers, leading to the development of new organizational structures that support effective collaboration. Things like

- Increased Productivity and Efficiency via automated, streamlined processes and reduced operational costs

- Job Transformation and Reskilling, as knowledge worker roles are automated, requiring human workers to focus on more complex and creative aspects of their functions

- Organizational Flexibility and Agility, as businesses will need to more quickly adapt to changing market conditions in their supply chains and identify and respond to customer needs through increase personalization and predictive marketing

Summary

In conclusion, it appears that this new technological wave will require some major changes in organizational roles and functions – as well as potentially profound structural social and economic changes in how we all work and live.

With a brief understanding of some of the organizational changes involved, now let's turn our attention to an old discipline that has taken on new significance in the Productivity Revolution: Data Governance.

CHAPTER 2

Data Governance: The Foundation for Generative AI

Data is vital for AI technical improvements. The use of AI to create more data enhances current capabilities and paves the way for future algorithmic improvements, especially on harder tasks.[1]

—A.I. Index Report 2024, Stanford University's Institute for Human-Centered Artificial Intelligence

One of the key takeaway messages from this book and this chapter is this: quality data is the key to everything.

Organizations embracing generative AI need to take managing data quality seriously. Generative AI, or for that matter, any type of data-driven processes, won't work if the predictions and assumptions are based on inaccuracies (low-quality data) and generalities (under-fitted or poorly designed models).

---

[1] A.I. Index Report 2024, Stanford University's Institute for Human-Centered Artificial Intelligence, p 15, https://aiindex.stanford.edu/report/

© Arthur J. O'Connor 2024
A. J. O'Connor, *Organizing for Generative AI and the Productivity Revolution*, https://doi.org/10.1007/979-8-8688-0959-0_2

Gen AI represents new challenges in Data Governance, but also new requirements to existing data quality and data engineering and management functions.

While this may seem obvious, the sad fact is that at most organizations, Data Governance is still a largely performative exercise, something to mention in presentations to the Board Audit Committee and Wall Street analysts. Sweeping, high-minded mission statements, QA compliance policies, and detailed procedures are created. Chief Data Officers and Data Stewards are appointed. Data Governance support functions are created. Yet all of this typically amounts to only superficial measures and simple data quality checks.

Now if your reaction to the above is: what actually do you mean by "Data Governance?" Then please continue reading the next section below, **"What's Data Governance?"**

If your reaction is: oh no…not again – another sermon on the importance of treating data as a strategic asset …blah, blah, blah. Please skip ahead to the chapter section entitled, **"What's Different About Data Governance with Generative AI**?" because some major changes are required. But just to be clear: this chapter is not a sermon. It's a call to action, as current best practices in Data Governance – considered as "nice to have's" in many organizations today – become essential requirements with generative AI.

And this chapter provides some useful tips on how to meet the many challenges involved.

What's Data Governance?

In essence, Data Governance is the modern-day version of a mix of interrelated functions that go by the names of Data Quality Control/ Assurance, Data Management, and, in the context of data protection, Information Security.

It's most commonly characterized by organizational structures, systems, and processes that define and enforce policies and procedures to protect and secure sensitive data (such as proprietary, confidential, and personally identifiable) information while also ensuring the quality, availability, and traceability of data whenever and wherever data are collected, moved, copied, analyzed, and shared.

Roles and Responsibilities

In this context, various roles and responsibilities have emerged:

- Executive Sponsor: An executive sponsor provides leadership and support for Data Governance initiatives, ensuring alignment with organizational goals and priorities. They champion the importance of Data Governance across the organization and allocate resources for its implementation.

- Steering Committee Members: The steering committee comprises stakeholders from different departments or business units responsible for overseeing Data Governance activities. They provide strategic guidance, define priorities, and resolve conflicts related to data management and usage.

- Data Owner: Data owners are individuals or teams responsible for the overall management and stewardship of specific datasets within the organization. They define data usage policies, ensure compliance with regulations, and oversee access controls and data quality.

- Data Stewards: Data stewards work closely with data owners to implement Data Governance policies and procedures. They are responsible for data classification, metadata management, data lineage, and resolving data-related issues or disputes.

- Data Auditors: Data audits involve regular assessments of data management practices and compliance with Data Governance policies. Audits help identify gaps or deficiencies in data management processes and ensure continuous improvement.

- Three Lines of Defense: The three lines of defense model delineates responsibilities for managing risks associated with data usage. The first line includes business units and data owners responsible for day-to-day data management. The second line comprises risk management and compliance functions that oversee Data Governance policies and controls. The third line involves internal audit or independent assurance functions that provide objective evaluations of Data Governance effectiveness.

Ideally, all three lines of defense work together to ensure compliance with all applicable data privacy laws and regulations, such as the General Data Protection Regulation (GDPR), California Consumer Privacy Act (CCPA), Gramm-Leach-Bliley Act (GLBA), Health Insurance Portability and Accountability Act (HIPAA), US Privacy Act of 1974, Children's Online Privacy Protection Act (COPPA), and Virginia Consumer Data Protection Act (CDPA). The penalty from federal and local authorities can be enormous for leakage of sensitive data as related to Personal Information (PI) and personally Identifiable Information(PII) - a reason why Data Loss Prevention (DLP) programs have taken center stage in Data Governance roles and responsibilities.

Key Role: Data Stewards

Data Stewards play a crucial role in ensuring the effective implementation of Data Governance within an organization – and thus are worthy of a more detailed description of their roles and responsibilities.

To fulfill their responsibilities effectively, Data Stewards need to have a comprehensive understanding of the organization's governance rules and policies, as well as the business contexts within which these rules and policies must be applied.

Firstly, knowledge of governance rules and policies enables Data Stewards to ensure compliance with regulatory requirements and organizational standards. They need to understand data privacy regulations, security protocols, data retention policies, and other relevant governance frameworks to ensure that data is managed and used in accordance with legal and ethical guidelines. By having a clear understanding of these rules and policies, Data Stewards can enforce data governance practices effectively and mitigate the risk of non-compliance.

Secondly, understanding the business contexts within which governance rules and policies must be applied is essential for Data Stewards to align data management practices with organizational objectives and priorities. They need to comprehend how different business units or departments use data, what data is critical for various business processes, and how data flows through the organization. This understanding allows Data Stewards to tailor governance rules and policies to meet the specific needs of different stakeholders and ensure that data management practices support organizational goals.

Moreover, Data Stewards play a critical role in guiding users of self-service technologies to apply governance and data quality standards effectively. Self-service technologies empower users to access and analyze data independently, but they also pose risks related to data quality, consistency, and compliance. Data Stewards can help users understand the importance of adhering to governance and data quality standards when using self-service tools.

Data Stewards can provide training and support to users, educating them about governance policies, data quality requirements, and best practices for data management. They can collaborate with IT teams to implement data governance controls within self-service technologies, such as data validation checks, access controls, and data lineage tracking. Additionally, Data Stewards can monitor data usage patterns and provide feedback to users on areas where governance and data quality standards may need improvement.

Principle of Least Privilege

A key concept in data security access management is the principle of least privilege (POLP) that aims to reduce the potential impact of security breaches by limiting users' access rights to only the minimum permissions necessary to perform their job functions.

This principle applies not only to users but also to applications, systems, and processes, ensuring that they have access only to the resources and data required for their intended purposes. By restricting access rights to the minimum necessary level, POLP helps minimize the potential damage that can result from unauthorized access or misuse of sensitive data.

Data Quality Metrics

Another important component to Data Governance is the use of metrics to evaluate data quality over time and compare the quality of different data sources to gain insights into the reliability, accuracy, completeness, and consistency of their data assets. Here's why and how organizations utilize metrics for evaluating data quality and prioritizing remediation efforts:

- Understanding Data Quality Trends: By tracking data quality metrics over time, organizations can identify trends, patterns, and anomalies in data quality performance. Monitoring metrics such as data accuracy, completeness, consistency, timeliness, and integrity allows organizations to assess how data quality evolves and fluctuates over different time periods. For example, organizations may observe seasonal variations in data quality, periodic spikes or dips in data accuracy, or long-term trends indicating gradual degradation or improvement in data quality. These insights help organizations understand the factors influencing data quality and prioritize remediation efforts accordingly.

- Benchmarking Data Sources: Metrics enable organizations to compare the quality of different data sources, systems, or processes against predefined benchmarks or industry standards. By establishing baseline metrics and performance targets, organizations can assess the relative quality of data from various sources and identify outliers or underperforming datasets. For instance, organizations may compare data quality metrics such as error rates, completeness percentages, or duplication rates across multiple data sources or systems. This comparative analysis helps administrators pinpoint areas of concern and allocate resources effectively to improve data quality where it is most needed.

- Identifying Data Quality Issues: Data quality metrics serve as diagnostic tools for identifying specific data quality issues, errors, or anomalies within datasets. Metrics provide quantitative insights into the nature and extent of data quality problems, enabling administrators to diagnose root causes and take corrective actions. For example, anomalies in data consistency metrics may indicate discrepancies or conflicts between data sources, while low completeness metrics may suggest missing or incomplete data records. By analyzing these metrics, administrators can prioritize remediation efforts and implement targeted interventions to address underlying data quality issues.

29

- Prioritizing Remediation Efforts: Metrics help organizations prioritize remediation efforts by quantifying the impact and severity of data quality issues and assessing their business implications. Administrators can use metrics to prioritize remediation based on factors such as data criticality, business impact, regulatory compliance requirements, and stakeholder priorities. For instance, high-impact data quality issues affecting mission-critical systems or regulatory reporting may be prioritized over lower-priority issues with minimal business impact. By aligning remediation efforts with strategic objectives and business priorities, organizations can optimize resource allocation and maximize the return on investment in data quality improvement initiatives.

- Driving Continuous Improvement: Data quality metrics support a culture of continuous improvement by providing feedback loops and performance benchmarks for monitoring progress and driving accountability. Organizations can use metrics to set goals, track performance against targets, and measure the effectiveness of data quality initiatives over time.

By establishing key performance indicators (KPIs) and monitoring progress against these metrics, organizations can identify areas for improvement, celebrate successes, and identify opportunities for further optimization.

This iterative approach to data quality management fosters a culture of data-driven decision-making and continuous improvement across the organization.

What's Different About Data Governance with Generative AI?

As organizations increasingly integrate LLMs into their operations to drive innovation, the importance of Data Governance grows exponentially – and not just because generative AI relies heavily on access to vast amounts of data, including internal proprietary data, to train and refine models.

Why the escalation in importance? We can think of three main reasons:

1. In addition to the established concerns of data integrity, compliance with data privacy regulations, and data security to prevent unauthorized access, there come new challenges in mitigating bias in training data and interpretable and responsible AI (we'll get into this topic in the next chapter).

2. New types of data models combining structured with unstructured[2] data, and new distributed data architectures require new strategies and approaches to data and metadata management.

3. Data flows in the petabyte (or millions of millions of bytes) scale require new and automated data acquisition and management architectures, as the current state of fragmented approaches and manual interventions across different data fiefdoms becomes impossible to manage.

---

[2] We find the term "unstructured data" a bit misleading, as it refers to data that doesn't fit neatly into a structured database format: things like text, images, videos, or audio recordings. While the data may seem chaotic, much "unstructured" data actually possesses underlying structure or patterns that can be discovered and utilized.

These data pipelines sometimes require extensive cleaning, missing data imputation, and munging (process of converting raw data into a more usable format) to normalize the data in a standardized format across the enterprise.

But perhaps the biggest reason is that, for most organizations, the stakes (risks and rewards) are so much higher.

In the past, when most data was used for off-line decision-support and reporting, most organizations could get by with "good enough" quality data. But "good enough" data is potentially disastrous when the results of data are used to make important decisions and drive mission-critical business processes like order fulfillment, supply chain optimization, quality control, or customer service – and/or when organizations sell their generated data to third parties, based on the promise of accuracy and efficacy.

Just consider the operational and reputational risk of hallucinations – false or misleading information presented as fact.

For the purposes of this chapter, we'll discuss a broad range of requirements, from new strategies and architectures for managing data and metadata, as well as the need for upgrading current practices.

Mitigating Bias in Training Data

A major concern and challenge in generative AI is migrating the risk of bias in training data. In essence: models trained on data reflecting biases will produce those same biases. Some strategies to consider:

Diverse Data Collection

- Ensure that your training dataset represents a wide range of demographics, backgrounds, and perspectives.

- Avoid underrepresentation: Pay attention to minority groups or less-represented classes to prevent bias.

Automated Preprocessing

- Instead of simple quality checks for missing values, misclassified fields, violation of data types and formats, use machine learning classification models to identify biases in your data, such as:

  - Balance class distribution: Oversample underrepresented classes or under-sampled overrepresented ones.

  - Remove irrelevant features: Eliminate features that introduce bias or are not relevant to the task.

Annotation Guidelines

- Clear guidelines: Provide annotators with explicit instructions on labeling data.

- Address potential biases: Highlight potential pitfalls related to bias during annotation.

Fair Sampling

- Stratified sampling: Ensure that each subgroup is well-represented in your training data.

- Adaptive sampling: Adjust sampling based on model performance to reduce bias.

Regularization Techniques

- Weighted loss functions: Assign different weights to different classes to balance their impact.

- Fairness-aware regularization: Penalize models for making biased predictions.

De-biasing Algorithms

- Adversarial training: Train a model to predict the protected attribute (e.g., gender) and minimize its influence on the main task.

- Reweighting instances: Adjust instance weights to reduce bias.

Post-processing

- Calibration: Adjust model predictions to ensure fairness across different groups.

- Threshold tuning: Set decision thresholds based on fairness considerations.

Evaluate Fairness Metrics

- Demographic parity: Compare outcomes across different groups.

- Equalized odds: Assess whether false positives/ negatives are balanced across groups.

- Disparate impact: Measure bias in decision outcomes.

Human Oversight and Intervention

- Review and iterate: Continuously assess model performance and address biases.

- Feedback from diverse stakeholders: Involve people from different backgrounds to provide insights.

Transparency and Documentation

- Document data collection and preprocessing: Maintain a record of decisions made during data preparation.

- Explainable AI: Use interpretable models to understand how decisions are made.

Retrieval Augmented Generation

One of the key advancements in AI techniques that has heightened the significance of Data Governance is Retrieval Augmented Generation (RAG). RAG combines retrieval-based methods with generative models to improve the relevance and coherence of generated outputs. While this technique enhances the capabilities of AI systems by enabling them to retrieve and synthesize information from vast repositories of data, it also introduces new challenges for Data Governance. Specifically, RAG necessitates careful management of the data used for retrieval to ensure its accuracy, relevance, and compliance with regulations and organizational policies.

This integration of proprietary data into AI systems enables organizations to create new business models, products, services, and processes that leverage the insights derived from this data-driven approach. However, with this integration comes the need for robust Data Governance practices to ensure the ethical, legal, and responsible use of data.

Access Controls

In the context of large language models (LLMs) and other AI systems, the principle of least privilege is equally important, albeit with some unique considerations. But for the principle to be effectively implemented with LLMs, an organization needs to adopt a more automated and streamlined process for creating, modifying, editing, and deleting user profiles and permission levels.

Again, we return to the theme that current best practices in Data Governance have become basic requirements in the age of LLMs.

In terms of security user profiles, it's a matter of not what, but how access controls should be implemented to ensure that only authorized personnel have access to the data used to train and fine-tune LLMs. This involves User Access Management Systems to house, maintain, and update roles and permissions based on job functions and responsibilities, to ensure access is granted only to those individuals who require it to perform their tasks effectively. Additionally, data encryption and anonymization techniques may be employed to further protect sensitive information and limit exposure to unauthorized users.

During the deployment and operation of LLMs, access controls should also be enforced to restrict interactions with the model to authorized applications and processes. This helps prevent malicious actors from exploiting vulnerabilities in the AI system to gain unauthorized access or manipulate its behavior. Access controls can include mechanisms such as authentication, authorization, and audit trails to monitor and control access to LLMs and the data they process.

Furthermore, the principle of least privilege extends beyond data access to encompass other aspects of LLM design and implementation, such as model architecture, APIs, and deployment environments. For example, developers should adhere to the principle of least privilege when designing APIs for interacting with LLMs, ensuring that only essential functionalities are exposed and that access is granted based on the principle of least privilege.

For more information, please refer to Appendix A – Data Governance Best Practices, which covers Metrics, Workflow Automation, Knowledge Graphs, Heterogeneous Data Architectures, and other important components to effective Data Governance.

Next we turn to changes in Corporate Governance that Gen AI adoption means for organizations.

CHAPTER 3

The Challenges to Corporate Governance

> I believe those creating, fueling and funding AI want, possibly unconsciously, to be God, and think on some level they *are* God.
>
> —Peggy Noonan, political columnist

As we all know, the potential for great upside often comes with the risk of significant downside. As organizations rush to harness and embed AI models in their core processes without the required organizational capabilities in place, they do so at great risk.

This chapter speaks to organizational functions and capabilities required to minimize the potential ethical, regulatory, legal, financial, and reputational risks that Gen AI systems hold for organizations, as well as strategies to maximize the return on these (often substantial) investments.

And yes, just like any other type of information system, Gen AI models can be vulnerable to adversarial attacks, data poisoning, or distributional shifts, leading to unreliable or erroneous outputs.

© Arthur J. O'Connor 2024
A. J. O'Connor, *Organizing for Generative AI and the Productivity Revolution*,
https://doi.org/10.1007/979-8-8688-0959-0_3

As noted previously, "Shadow AI" systems can present a major challenge to system integration and data consistency. Unauthorized systems may not be designed to integrate with existing IT infrastructure, leading to data silos and inconsistencies. This can compromise the accuracy and reliability of AI-driven insights and decisions and can also make it difficult for organizations to maintain a single source of truth. Without proper controls and safeguards, these systems can potentially disrupt existing IT operations, compromise data integrity, and even cause system failures.

And as we've noted in the previous chapter, user access management is another critical area of concern. Unauthorized AI systems may not have the same level of security and access controls as authorized systems, potentially exposing sensitive data to unauthorized users. And of course, data privacy and information security are major risks in the age of AI, as these systems, which are trained on massive datasets, can potentially compromise an organization's commitment to protecting personal data.

In addition to these generic areas of IT risk management, however, there are specific types of challenges posed by Gen AI systems to Corporate Governance.

What's Different About Gen AI

As we will see in Chapter 7, Gen AI systems may be subject to various industry-specific regulations, data protection laws, and ethical guidelines. To comply with new regulations, such as the EU's Artificial Intelligence Act, organizations should ensure that they have a clear understanding of the requirements and implications of these regulations. This includes conducting regular risk assessments to identify potential compliance risks, as well as implementing policies and procedures to ensure that all AI systems are developed and deployed in compliance with relevant regulations and standards.

These risks can have serious consequences, particularly in areas such as hiring, lending, and law enforcement, where AI is increasingly being used to make critical decisions.

Gen AI models often lack interpretability and transparency, especially proprietary or "closed" models, which operate as "black boxes," making it difficult to understand their decision-making processes and logic.

This lack of interpretability and transparency makes it challenging to audit and verify the model's outputs, potentially leading to unexpected or biased results. It also complicates the identification and mitigation of potential risks or vulnerabilities.

Here are some important topics and strategies to consider.

Ethical AI

Organizations must ensure that all AI systems, whether authorized or not, are developed and deployed in a responsible and ethical manner and that their decisions and predictions can be easily understood and explained. This requires a shift toward more transparent and explainable AI models, as well as the establishment of robust AI ethics policies and guidelines.

Here are a few common organizational practices and procedures that can help mitigate the risks:[1]

- Establish an AI Governance Framework: An AI governance framework provides guidelines and policies for the development, deployment, and use of AI systems within an organization. This framework should include clear definitions of roles and responsibilities, procedures for AI system development and deployment, and guidelines for data management and security.

---

[1] Yes, we realize there's overlap from some of the functions listed in the previous chapter on Data Governance, but we feel a lot of this stuff bears repeating.

- Implement AI System Inventory and Monitoring: Organizations should maintain an inventory of all AI systems in use, including both authorized and unauthorized systems. This inventory should be regularly updated and monitored to detect any new or unauthorized systems. Organizations can use automated tools to scan their networks and identify AI systems in use.

- Conduct Regular Risk Assessments: Regular risk assessments can help organizations identify potential risks associated with shadow AI systems. These assessments should evaluate the potential impact of these systems on data privacy, information security, system integration, and other areas.

- Provide Training and Awareness Programs: Training and awareness programs can help employees understand the risks associated with shadow AI and the importance of adhering to AI governance policies. These programs should cover topics such as data privacy, information security, and responsible AI use.

- Implement Data Governance Policies: As noted previously, Data Governance policies should ensure that all AI systems are developed and deployed using high-quality, unbiased, and representative datasets. These policies should also address data privacy and security concerns and should establish clear guidelines for data management and sharing.

- Implement Access Controls and Monitoring: Access controls and monitoring can help prevent unauthorized access to AI systems and data. Organizations should implement role-based access controls and monitor user activity to detect any suspicious or unauthorized activity.

- Establish Production Environment Controls: Organizations should establish clear policies and procedures for deploying AI systems into production environments. These policies should include requirements for testing, validation, and monitoring and should ensure that AI systems do not disrupt existing IT operations.

- Implement Security Measures: Organizations should implement robust security measures to protect AI systems and data from cyber threats and data breaches. These measures should include regular security audits, vulnerability assessments, and penetration testing.

- Promote Responsible and Interpretable AI: Organizations should promote responsible and interpretable AI by developing and deploying AI systems that are transparent, explainable, and fair. This requires a shift toward more transparent and explainable AI models, as well as the establishment of robust AI ethics policies and guidelines.

Corporations deploying Gen AI are increasingly deploying Corporate IT Governance internal automated continuous audit mechanisms. Gen AI output in many cases are passed through these audit systems before use in production and support.

Detecting and Controlling for Bias

And, as noted in the previous chapter, AI systems may be developed using biased or incomplete datasets, which can lead to inaccurate predictions and decision-making.

Gen AI models can inherit and amplify biases present in their training data, leading to discriminatory or unfair decisions. Addressing these biases and ensuring ethical and responsible AI deployment is a complex task, requiring robust governance frameworks and continuous monitoring.

To mitigate this risk, organizations must implement robust data governance policies that ensure all AI systems, whether authorized or not, are developed using unbiased and representative datasets, as described in the previous chapter. Note that variances in training data and inference data are a major concern in Gen AI, which is why organizations are implementing continuous monitoring controls to detect bias and variance.

Autonomous and/or Intelligent Agents

Another trend that presents IT risks for organizations is the growing use of virtual agents for automating tasks. While virtual agents can provide significant benefits in terms of efficiency and productivity, they can also pose risks in terms of data privacy and security.

To mitigate these risks, organizations should implement robust security measures, such as encryption and secure communication protocols, to protect data transmitted between virtual agents and other systems. Organizations should also ensure that virtual agents are properly configured and monitored to prevent unauthorized access or misuse.

Copyright Infringement Risks

How can one ensure output from a foundation model doesn't contain copyrighted material? There is no sure-fire way, but there are a few approaches that can help mitigate the risk of generating copyrighted content with a large language model or other generative AI system:

1. Filtering and Detection

    – Implement filters to detect potential copyright violations in the generated text based on similarity measures against existing copyrighted works.

    – Use plagiarism detection tools and databases to identify matches with copyrighted material during or after generation.

    – Apply watermarking techniques to trace the origin of generated text.

2. Controlled Training Data

    – Carefully curate and filter the training data to exclude copyrighted material as much as possible.

    – Use public domain, Creative Commons, and other freely licensed data sources for training.

    – Implement legal data sourcing and licensing processes.

3. Model Adjustments

    – Adjust the model architecture, hyper-parameters, or fine-tuning approaches to reduce the likelihood of reproducing memorized training examples verbatim.

- Explore techniques like retrieval-augmented generation to separate knowledge retrieval from generation.

4. Output Filtering and Editing

- Implement post-processing steps to detect and remove potential copyright violations from the generated output.

- Provide human oversight and editing to review and refine the generated content.

5. Secured APIs and Permissions

- Implement access controls and authentication for generative AI APIs to prevent unauthorized use.

- Obtain necessary permissions and licenses for commercial use of copyrighted material, if required.

6. Legal and Ethical Considerations

- Consult legal experts to understand copyright laws and fair use guidelines in your jurisdiction.

- Establish clear policies and guidelines for responsible and ethical use of generative AI systems.

- Provide transparency about the model's capabilities and limitations regarding copyright issues.

It's important to note that while these measures can help mitigate the risk, they may not completely eliminate the possibility of generating copyrighted content, especially in cases where the model has inadvertently memorized and reproduced copyrighted material during training.

Security of Internal Proprietary Data and Intellectual Property

Conversely, one might then wonder, how can one ensure use of a foundation model doesn't result in leakage of internal proprietary data or an organization's Intellectual Property?

The trend toward custom local models that are trained on internal and often proprietary data or sensitive personal information presents both opportunities and risks for organizations. On the one hand, these models can be fine-tuned for specific tasks and can provide significant benefits in terms of accuracy and efficiency. On the other hand, they can also pose significant risks, particularly in terms of data privacy and security.

One of the risks associated with using custom local models is the potential for feeding trade secrets or other confidential information to train a publicly facing AI model. This risk is particularly relevant when using Retrieval Augmented Generation (RAG) to access relevant information. RAG is a technique that involves using a neural network to retrieve relevant information from a large corpus of text and then using that information to generate a response. If the corpus of text includes confidential or proprietary information, there is a risk that this information could be inadvertently disclosed through the AI model.

To mitigate this risk, organizations should implement robust data governance policies that ensure that all data used to train AI models is properly classified and protected. This includes implementing access controls and monitoring to prevent unauthorized access to sensitive data, as well as using techniques such as differential privacy to protect confidential information.

Ensuring that the use of a foundation model does not result in leakage of internal proprietary data or intellectual property (IP) is a critical concern, especially for organizations dealing with sensitive information. Here are some strategies that can be employed:

1. Sanitize and Anonymize Training Data

    –   Thoroughly review and sanitize any internal data used for training or fine-tuning the foundation model.

    –   Remove or anonymize any proprietary information, trade secrets, personally identifiable information (PII), or other sensitive data from the training set.

    –   Implement robust data anonymization techniques, such as masking, tokenization, or use of pseudonyms. A popular method is Format Preserving Encryption, which uses a set of Public and Private Keys. For example, the social security number 123456789 is replaced with a number of the same format (like 567345687), which the end user can decrypt to 123456789.

2. Secure Model Access and Deployment

    –   Restrict access to the foundation model and its training data to authorized personnel only.

    –   Deploy the model in a secure and isolated environment, such as a private cloud or on-premises infrastructure.

    –   Implement strong access controls, authentication, and encryption measures.

3. Monitor and Audit Model Outputs

   – Implement monitoring and auditing mechanisms to detect potential data leaks in the model's outputs.

   – Use techniques like watermarking, fingerprinting, or traitor tracing to identify the source of any leaked data.

   – Regularly review and analyze the model's outputs for potential IP or data leakage.

4. Establish Robust Policies and Procedures

   – Develop and enforce clear policies and procedures for the responsible use of foundation models within the organization.

   – Provide thorough training and awareness programs for employees on data privacy, security, and IP protection.

   – Implement incident response and mitigation plans in case of any data leakage incidents.

5. Secure Model Updates and Versioning

   – Establish secure processes for updating and versioning the foundation model.

   – Ensure that any updated or fine-tuned models do not inadvertently introduce new data leakage risks.

   – Maintain a secure and auditable version control system for model updates.

6.   Contractual Agreements and Legal Compliance

-   If using third-party foundation models or services, carefully review and negotiate contractual agreements to ensure IP protection and data privacy clauses are in place.

-   Comply with relevant data protection regulations, such as GDPR, CCPA, or industry-specific regulations.

-   Consult legal experts and data protection officers to ensure compliance with applicable laws and regulations.

7.   Continuous Monitoring and Improvement

-   Regularly review and update data protection and IP safeguards as new threats or vulnerabilities emerge.

-   Stay informed about the latest research and best practices in secure and privacy-preserving machine learning.

-   Continuously improve the organization's data governance and security posture.

It's important to note that while these strategies can significantly reduce the risk of data leakage, they may not eliminate the risk entirely. Therefore, ongoing vigilance, risk assessment, and continuous improvement are necessary to protect proprietary data and IP when using foundation models.

Organizational Readiness

Often overlooked is the task of aligning human talent with the organizational functions and capabilities required to succeed – a topic we'll tackle in Part II of this book.

Integrating Gen AI systems into existing mission-critical processes and systems often requires significant changes in workflows, organizational structures, and mindsets. Managing this change effectively, addressing resistance to adoption, and ensuring proper training and support for stakeholders can be a significant challenge.

To address gaps in skill sets, many organizations will require employee to "upskill." Fortunately, there are many outlets and opportunities to do that.

And perhaps most importantly, organizations will need to assess and match skills sets and personas with new types of roles and responsibilities (again, more on this later in the book).

10-Point Checklist

Below is a checklist of functions that executives should ask: (1) whether their organization has a governance function, (2) what specific activities it conducts, (3) how its performance is measured, (4) what are the results, and (5) how well do those results compare with best practices or at least industry standards.

1. Governance Framework

    – Develop a governance framework that outlines the principles, policies, and guidelines for the responsible development, deployment, and use of Gen AI systems.

- Involve cross-functional stakeholders, including IT, risk management, legal, ethics, and business teams, in the governance process.

- Define clear roles, responsibilities, and accountability for each stakeholder group.

2. Risk Assessments

- Perform thorough risk assessments to identify and prioritize potential risks associated with Gen AI systems, such as data privacy, security, ethical concerns, regulatory compliance, and model reliability.

- Assess the impact and likelihood of these risks on mission-critical processes and systems.

- Develop risk mitigation strategies and contingency plans to address identified risks.

3. Data Management

- Establish rigorous data governance processes to ensure the quality, security, and privacy of data used for training and deploying Gen AI models.

- Implement data anonymization, encryption, and access control measures to protect sensitive or proprietary data.

- Develop processes for data lineage tracking and traceability to enable auditing and accountability.

4. Model Interpretability and Transparency

    –   Explore techniques such as explainable AI (XAI), model interpretability, and interpretable model architectures to improve the transparency and interpretability of Gen AI systems.

    –   Implement model monitoring and auditing mechanisms to detect and address potential biases, errors, or inconsistencies.

5. Model Reliability and Robustness

    –   Implement rigorous testing and validation processes to ensure the reliability and robustness of Gen AI models, including adversarial testing and stress testing.

    –   Develop strategies for model updating, versioning, and monitoring to maintain model performance and address potential vulnerabilities or distributional shifts.

6. Regulatory Compliance and Ethical Alignment

    –   Establish processes to continuously monitor and comply with relevant regulations, industry standards, and ethical guidelines related to AI systems.

    –   Implement ethical AI principles and frameworks to ensure fairness, accountability, and transparency in the development and deployment of Gen AI systems.

7. Collaboration and Knowledge Sharing

   – Encourage cross-functional collaboration and knowledge sharing among IT, risk management, legal, ethics, and business teams throughout the Gen AI system lifecycle.

   – Provide regular training and awareness programs to upskill employees and stakeholders on Gen AI risks, best practices, and governance processes.

8. Continuous Monitoring and Improvement

   – Establish processes for continuous monitoring, auditing, and reporting of Gen AI system performance, risks, and compliance.

   – Regularly review and update governance policies, risk mitigation strategies, and ethical frameworks to adapt to evolving Gen AI technologies and industry best practices.

9. Third-Party Expertise and Resources

   – Collaborate with industry associations, regulatory bodies, and external experts to stay informed about best practices, emerging risks, and governance frameworks for Gen AI systems.

   – Consider leveraging third-party risk management and compliance services or tools to supplement internal capabilities.

10. Measure and Optimize Return on Investment (ROI)

   – Establish clear Key Performance Indicators (KPIs) and metrics to measure the business value and ROI of Gen AI system investments.

– Continuously evaluate and optimize the performance, efficiency, and effectiveness of Gen AI systems in mission-critical processes to maximize ROI.

Summary

As we see, the adoption of Gen AI technologies will require a new set of roles, functions, and capabilities required to minimize the potential ethical, regulatory, legal, financial, and reputational risks that Gen AI systems hold for organizations.

In the next (Part II) section of this book, we'll turn to the key differences and successful attributes of key players – and some of the inherent conflicts with other types of players – in the design, implementation, and support of advanced foundation models.

PART II

Organizational Transformation: Current and Future States

CHAPTER 4

Lessons Learned

(...failed attempts, words of wisdom, and success stories)

> *An important thing to realize about the grandest conversations surrounding AI is that, most of the time, everyone is making things up.*[1]

—Charlie Warzel, writer

To recap, in the Introduction, we raised some organizational behavioral issues associated with Gen AI adoption and described the key purpose of this book, and in Part I provided some context in the history of workplace automation, and some of the changes in roles and functions already taking place.

In the first three chapters, we touched upon many themes, starting with the incredible potential of generative models to create original material from the vast repositories of human knowledge – with the capability, thanks to their pre-training and alignment, to create the illusion to users that the models actually understand what they're saying – the so-called "ELIZA effect."[2]

---

[1] "AI Has Become a Technology of Faith," Charlie Warzel, The Atlantic, July 2024, https://www.msn.com/en-us/health/other/ai-has-become-a-technology-of-faith/ar-BB1pT3wE?ocid=hpmsn&cvid=35cfe42e01fd44dc819f6933159fb639&ei=25

[2] https://en.wikipedia.org/wiki/ELIZA_effect

Moreover, this technology offers the promise of unprecedented empowerment of users: a future when no one needs to learn how to write computer code, be able to draw illustrations, produce videos, write essays, or compose music. All they need to do is state their deepest desires to the seemingly all-powerful Gen AI genie, who immediately grants their wish. The only limits are their own imaginations.

And let's not forget the superhuman decision-making potential of compound intelligent agents, or Agentic AI, in which each agent functions independently yet collaboratively within the system, gathering information about its environment to assess and analyze situations and make reasoned observations and decisions from interpreting the relationship between goals, perception, collaboration, execution outcomes.

Just think of the possibilities of new/disruptive business models!

But we also stressed that with this incredible creative empowerment of workers comes significant challenges (notably the risks of "Shadow AI" and hallucinations), which will most likely result in profound changes in organizational roles, responsibilities, structures, and behaviors.

As a prime example of this organizational evolution, we cited the trend at many firms that are integrating their (once separate and distinct) Application Development and Site Operations functions into units of both software architects and system engineers into DevOps, and still newer organizational functions called "ML Ops" to more effectively manage the important differences in traditional software deployment vs. machine learning model design and development.

In Part II, we turn to the topic of the future transformation of organizations and leadership skills, as Gen AI adoption reshapes organizational structures and the expanded/changing roles within them. In this chapter, we talk with leading industry practitioners, journalists, and academic researchers in artificial intelligence to get their take on the current application of Gen AI across a broad range of fields.

Failed Attempts

So let's start this chapter on some items that might fall under the category of failed attempts, or what **not** to do, from examples of earlier uses of algorithmic and Gen AI models:

- Air Canada's chatbot on its website hallucinated, falsely informing a passenger that it offered bereavement fares retroactively. When the airline denied the discount, the passenger sued, and in small claims court presented a screenshot of the chatbot's response. The court found in favor of the passenger, who was awarded $812.02 in damages and court fees.[3]

- A Harvard Business Review article found that most hiring algorithms – often believed to be objective, color-blind decision aids for hiring managers - can automatically reject a significant proportion of qualified non-white candidates, given the history of hiring managers, who are predominantly white, to prefer hiring white candidates – a behavioral bias embedded in the massive datasets these models are trained on.[4]

---

[3] "What Air Canada Lost In 'Remarkable' Lying AI Chatbot Case," Forbes, Marisa Garcia, Feb 19, 2024 https://www.forbes.com/sites/marisagarcia/2024/02/19/what-air-canada-lost-in-remarkable-lying-ai-chatbot-case/

[4] "All the Ways Hiring Algorithms Can Introduce Bias," Harvard Business Review, Miranda Bogen
  May 06, 2019 https://hbr.org/2019/05/all-the-ways-hiring-algorithms-can-introduce-bias

- In a similar case of training data bias, a non-profit news organization's investigation found that underwriting algorithms used some mortgage banks were more likely to deny home loans to people of color (80% for Blacks, 40% for Latinos, and 70% for Native Americans) than for white applicants of the same credit worthiness.[5]

- In 2023, a judge discovered the legal brief filed by two New York lawyers contained six fictional case citations generated by an AI tool's hallucinations. In imposing a sanctions order, the judge noted that there was nothing "inherently improper" in lawyers using AI to assist in research but that ethics rules "impose a gatekeeping role on attorneys to ensure the accuracy of their filings." [6]

What are the lessons learned from these examples? There are reminders of the dangers of over-reliance on models and the age-old dictum, "GIGO" (garbage in, garbage out), still holds true.

And implementing Gen AI on an enterprise scale poses even greater challenges.

---

[5] "A.I. Bias Caused 80% Of Black Mortgage Applicants To Be Denied," Forbes, Kori Hale,

Contributor, Sep 2, 2021 https://www.forbes.com/sites/korihale/2021/09/02/ai-bias-caused-80-of-black-mortgage-applicants-to-be-denied/

[6] "New York lawyers sanctioned for using fake ChatGPT cases in legal brief," Reuters, Sara Merken

June 26, 2023, https://www.reuters.com/legal/new-york-lawyers-sanctioned-using-fake-chatgpt-cases-legal-brief-2023-06-22/

Words of Wisdom: A Cautionary Tale from an AI Executive at a Large, Global Bank

An Executive Director of AI and Innovation at one of the world's largest banks explains some of the fundamental challenges large, global organizations face when adopting Gen AI.

"I've seen so many companies get into AI for the wrong reasons," he begins.

Many decision-makers, the financial services industry veteran notes, fall victim to the herd mentality and rush off with a big dollar proposal to the board, make a flashy presentation to Wall Street investment research analysts, issue press releases crowing about this bold new strategy, appoint a Chief AI Officer, create a Center of Excellence to "build the knowledge base," and hire a small army of data scientists and data engineers – with no thought or mention of return on investment.

"Any time I heard the phrase that some major initiative is a 'journey, not a destination' I think of the Lewis Carroll quote, 'If you don't know where you're going, any road will take you there.'"

"Unless you have a specific set of use cases and a well-defined plan or a coherent strategy," he cautions, "undertaking an enterprise-wide Gen AI initiative amounts to burning a large pile of cash."

One of the key barriers to success that he's witnessed in his own organization is that most large organizations are not design structured for managing their data on an enterprise scale. "Most organizations don't seem to think it through of what it takes to unlock the value of their data," he adds.

Why Managing Data for AI Is So Difficult

As we've noted in this book, both machine learning and generative AI models require vast amounts of quality data on which to train models, but most organizations are not capable of harnessing their data to make it available on that scale.

One of the biggest challenges, this executive says, is that owners of the data don't have the financial resources to make the data discoverable across organizational silos, which is the first step to finding out whether datasets are of any value. This is particularly challenging when the scope of work is on a global scale.

The overarching problem, the banking executive maintains, is that, at too many companies, "data is the necessary evil to do business; it's not treated as a first-class citizen."

"We've got over 170 petabytes of data, growing at about 15 to 20 percent a year, located at over 100 data centers, stored in about 125,000 databases – most tied to specific applications. Across all these silos, we don't have a unified schema to know what all this data are; the information isn't discoverable."

"For example, consider credit card transactions," he adds. "Why do we keep this information? One of the big reasons is that by regulation we have to. We store in transaction processing systems and OLAP (online analytical processing) databases so that we can perform simple multi-dimensional analytical queries for business reporting. And then, in response to business user requests, we provide different views of the data, make different copies (and copies of copies) of the data, and create exposures and abstractions of the data for various different reasons...but we don't which versions are stale, incomplete, duplicative, inaccurate or their context," he says.

"How can you catalog all that data, growing so fast, in so many different formats and versions, across so many platforms?" he asked rhetorically. He notes that vendor data management vendors aren't always the right solution. "Yes, there are vendors who offer platforms to address this problem – but the different platforms don't talk to each other."

So it seems while users of the data in the lines of business want completely accurate, clean, and well-managed data, the individual owners of the data in IT don't have the budget, financial incentive, or organizational authority to ensure this level of quality and transparency. Those brave souls who undertake the task to make data discoverable on an ad hoc basis – clarify and document the schema, create the traceability, and validate the quality - quickly realize how slow, manual, expensive, and painful this process is.

In other words, neither the people who own nor use the data have the resources or incentive to realize the full value of the data. "Organizational roles have not yet evolved in most organizations to handle this," he concludes.

At this point, the reader might logically ask: okay, so how does an organization unlock the full value of data? The answer, already well-known in the data provider business, is that you manage it like a product.

As defined by McKinsey, "A data product delivers a high-quality, ready-to-use set of data that people across an organization can easily access and apply to different business challenges."[7] We talk about the trend in companies' "productizing" or "monetizing" their data later in this chapter.

Disparate Development Cycles and Processes

As we've noted in our discussions about "ML Ops," the model development cycle is fundamentally different from traditional software development – which at most organizations, this executive maintains, is still not well understood.

So one of the biggest challenges for organizations to embrace Gen AI is departmental and functional friction. Some of this friction can be attributed to the lack of understanding about processes and controls.

"In most software development projects, it takes 9 to 12 months to produce the application. In ML and Gen AI, it's more like a few weeks. But it takes three to four months to get approvals to get the data," the banking exec notes.

---

[7] "How to unlock the full value of data? Manage it like a product," Veeral Desai, Tim Fountaine, and Kayvaun Rowshankish McKinsey, June 14, 2022. https://www.mckinsey.com/capabilities/quantumblack/our-insights/how-to-unlock-the-full-value-of-data-manage-it-like-a-product

He explains that in software development, there's different datasets used with different levels of controls around them. Development environments use mock data, with relatively simple controls over them; test environments use production-like data that is masked or otherwise anonymized, with more stringent controls; and production environments have full sets of rigorous controls.

But models need production data, but the controls that are associated with production data often represent overkill, as model design is inherently experimental – few models actually make it to production. As a result, time, effort, and money go to waste.

So how do firms bypass that unnecessary expenditure? Some use Gen AI models to create "synthetic data" that mimics the traits of production data (but again you need production data in the first place to create synthetic data). But the standard way of dealing with this problem, at least in large corporations, is to file "risk acceptances" (an extremely manual, lengthy often paper-based process) to negotiate a waiver of controls, with some type of justification as "Well, we're simply training a model; we're not testing software for deployment." And sometimes this works; sometimes it doesn't.

The bottom line is that most organizations are still a long way off in developing a rational, efficient full-stack development approach for model design and deployment, he asserts.

Key Decision: Moving Compute to Data or Data to Compute
According to this executive, the fundamental decision most organizations need to resolve in embracing Gen AI is whether to bring GPUs to the data or bring data to the GPUs. Translation: either build the computational power on premises to access the organization's legacy data stores, or migrate the data to the cloud where it can be where it can be fed into cloud-based LLM platforms available via Amazon Web Services, Google Cloud, or Microsoft's Azure.

This executive has seen this struggle play out in his own organization, and the results weren't pretty. But the underlying cause of the problem had little to do with Gen AI.

He cites as the main reason for the decision to bring data to compute was largely to address the current problems with the on-premise legacy computing infrastructure.

"Our network is a mess. Our global network of ATM's in our branches are on the same network as employee workstations. I can ping a cash machine anywhere in the world from my desktop!"

Aside from the lack of segregation of computing environments, he notes, is massive inefficiency. He estimates that about one-third of the data centers' capacity is used to host VDI cards that emulate personal computers, for which users use only about 60% of the functionality when one considers most employees spend the majority of their working time in Microsoft 365. And many legacy mainframe applications remain written in ancient languages such as FORTRAN and COBOL.

His point: the migration to the cloud was never about enabling users to access advanced LLMs; it was about cleaning up long-standing issues with the legacy infrastructure – and money. Achieving an annual cost of only 25% for an organization with an annual $10 billion IT budget means $2.5 billion in annual savings. But migrating data to the cloud raised all kinds of financial, technical (many applications need to be re-written), operational, risk and control, and ethical issues.

Risk and Controls

Lastly, he also noted that auditors and regulators, not unlike senior management, have yet to come to grips with Gen AI and model development in general. He points to banking regulations that require financial institutions to maintain a risk-rated inventory of models, in order to assign various controls and tests for the higher-risk models.

That sounds reasonable, but there's no standard definition of what a model is, or how it differs from simple formulas in spreadsheets, that is, no clear distinction between a (high-risk) model and a (lower-risk) "analytical tool." He tells a story of how the firm's equity trading systems using reinforcement learning for trade execution were classified as an "analytical tool" because they include a pop-up to ask the trader whether or not to proceed with executing the trade.

Success Stories

Thankfully, organizations are moving up the learning curve and getting better at improving data quality, fine-tuning their models, writing more specific and effective prompts, and minimizing the risk of hallucinations by grounding prompts with context-specific data.

Here are some successful examples of common-sense implementations, grouped by function (albeit on a smaller, more use-case-focused scale).

Content Creation

The Washington Post developed its own AI tool, Heliograf, to scan and analyze vast amounts of election results simultaneously, enabling its reporters and editors to generate timely news coverage on House, Senate, and gubernatorial races for all 50 states – nearly 500 races in total.[8]

BuzzFeed's "Infinity Quizzes," named for the infinite number of outputs it can generate, creates unique and personalized quizzes for readers based on inputs from BuzzFeed staff writers and audience member's contributions.[9]

---

[8] "The Washington Post to use artificial intelligence to cover nearly 500 races on Election Day," WashPostPR, October 19, 2016 https://www.washingtonpost.com/pr/wp/2016/10/19/the-washington-post-uses-artificial-intelligence-to-cover-nearly-500-races-on-election-day/

[9] "BuzzFeed Unveils New Content Format 'Infinity Quizzes' Powered By AI Revolutionizing The Internet's Favorite Quiz," BuzzFeedPress, Feb 14, 2023 https://www.buzzfeed.com/buzzfeedpress/buzzfeed-unveils-new-content-format-infinity-quizzes

Customer Service

Bank of America's AI virtual assistant for mobile banking, Erica, provides customers a holistic view of their liquidity – cash flow, account balances, transaction history, and upcoming bills – as well as personalized financial advice, based on these inputs.[10]

The ride share company Lyft uses AI chatbots to generate faster, more accurate routes, more convenient pickup spots, and even predict where customers most likely want to go, based on recent trends.[11]

Product Design and Development

Nike created its own generative AI model based on data on athletes' preferences to create hundreds of images that Nike designers then synthesize and prototype using 3D sketching and printing to create customized and innovative footwear.[12]

Architecture, engineering, and construction software firm Autodesk developed its Autodesk Fusion generative design AI to help engineers and designers explore design possibilities that may not have been considered otherwise by generating countless permutations, potentially leading to more efficient and creative solutions.[13]

---

[10] "Erica® is here for you, your life and your goals." Bank of America, `https://promotions.bankofamerica.com/digitalbanking/mobilebanking/erica`

[11] "How Lyft uses AI to get you where you want to go, faster," Sarah Conlisk, Inside Lyft, Aug 10, 2023 `https://www.lyft.com/blog/posts/how-lyft-uses-ai-to-get-you-where-you-want-to-go-faster`

[12] "Nike developing AI model as part of design 'step change," Dezeen, Nat Barker, May 7 2024 `https://www.dezeen.com/2024/05/07/nike-ai-model-john-hoke/`

[13] "Generative design AI," Autodesk, `https://www.autodesk.com/solutions/generative-design-ai-software`

Human Resources

Unilever, Hilton, and Goldman Sachs use AI to screen resumes and conduct initial interview stages to identify the most qualified candidates, streamline the hiring process, and reduce bias.[14]

Financial Services

JPMorgan Chase developed its COIN (Contract Intelligence) platform to review legal documents in seconds – work that once required 360,000 hours of manual work each year by lawyers and loan officers.[15]

Goldman Sachs employs AI for financial forecasting and risk management, analyzing vast amounts of trading data in real time, helping the firm to identify and manage market risk faster and more effectively.[16]

Healthcare

Healthcare technology solutions Zebra Medical Vision uses AI to analyze medical imaging data, providing radiologists with insights and enabling early detection of cancer and cardiovascular diseases.[17]

---

[14] "How Unilever, Hilton, Goldman Sachs & more leverage AI to find top talent faster & reduce bias,"
mTestHub, April 18, 2024 https://www.linkedin.com/pulse/how-unilever-hilton-goldman-sachs-more-leverage-ai-find-top-talent-t18me/

[15] "JPMorgan Chase uses tech to save 360,000 hours of annual work by lawyers and loan officers," Debra Cassens Weiss, ABA Journal, March 2, 2017 https://www.abajournal.com/news/article/jpmorgan_chase_uses_tech_to_save_360000_hours_of_annual_work_by_lawyers_and

[16] "Leveraging AI in Electronic Trading: A Game Changer for Investment Banks," Electronic Trading Technology, June 26, 2023 https://sissoftwarefactory.com/blog/leveraging-ai-in-electronic-trading-a-game-changer-for-investment-banks/

[17] "Zebra Medical Vision: transforming patient care through AI," Vartan Pahalyants, Digital Data Design Institute at Harvard, April 21, 2021 https://d3.harvard.edu/platform-digit/submission/zebra-medical-vision-transforming-patient-care-through-ai/

IBM Watson Health enables healthcare providers to leverage huge datasets to provide personalized treatment plans specifically customized to individual patients' medical conditions.[18]

Supply Chain and Logistics

UPS developed ORION (On-Road Integrated Optimization and Navigation), an AI-powered route optimization tool, to improve delivery efficiency and reduce fuel consumption.[19]

Walmart uses AI to predict demand for products, optimizing inventory management to ensure that the right amount of stock is available when needed.[20]

In addition to these examples, here are some firsthand accounts on how organizations are leveraging the power of Gen AI.

Improving Patient Care and Claims Processing

Javier Guillen, Director of Data and AI Solutions at Microsoft, believes that great changes are on the horizon for generative AI, particularly within the healthcare sector.

---

[18] "IBM Creates Watson Health to Analyze Medical Data," Steve Lohr, New York Times, April 13, 2015 https://archive.nytimes.com/bits.blogs.nytimes.com/2015/04/13/ibm-creates-watson-health-to-analyze-medical-data/

[19] "UPS To Enhance ORION With Continuous Delivery Route Optimization," UPS, Jan 29, 2020. https://about.ups.com/us/en/newsroom/press-releases/innovation-driven/ups-to-enhance-orion-with-continuous-delivery-route-optimization.html#

[20] "Walmart Commerce Technologies Launches AI-Powered Logistics Product," Walmart, March 14, 2024 https://corporate.walmart.com/news/2024/03/14/walmart-commerce-technologies-launches-ai-powered-logistics-product

Guillen notes that healthcare providers are investigating the use of LLM-based chatbots to consolidate operational and clinical data and streamline workflows. For instance, AI can potentially be used to facilitate shift transitions for nurses by compiling necessary patient information from various sources into a concise summary, thereby saving time, which is crucial for emergency department staff at the start of their shifts.

He also highlights ongoing trials by healthcare providers and insurers to refine claim processing – a longstanding challenge due to the varied coding and processing methods across the industry. LLMs offer a potential solution by standardizing procedures and supporting claim agents with real-time assistance, simplifying the complexity of claim reconciliation and enhancing the efficiency of the revenue capture process.

A New Way to Solve the Accountant Shortage

Mark Maurer, a reporter at *The Wall Street Journal* who covers corporate finance and accounting, sees CFOs and their staffs increasing experimentation with AI tools to validate invoices, detect financial fraud in large datasets of transactions, and forecast future finances.

Yet, in terms of widespread adoption, he hears this common refrain from them: "It's early days."

Maurer admits this is not surprising, given the personality profile of CFOs. "They tend to be highly risk-adverse," he notes. A recent study by SAP bears this out. In a survey of financial leaders, only 4% said they have a "strong" grasp of AI. "CFOs are pushing ahead with deploying AI, but admit their knowledge is highly limited."[21]

---

[21] "CFO Insights Report: Repositioning for Growth," SAP/Concur, https://www.concur.com/sites/default/files/ww_en_rpt_all_cfo_insights_repositioning_for_growth_imcc_20240315_rc.pdf

But Maurer does see Gen AI as a near-term solution for a chronic problem: the growing shortage of accountants, as fewer students are pursuing degrees in accounting and entering the field.[22]

He reported that several publicly held firms - auto-parts provider Advance Auto Parts, electric-air-taxi firm Joby Aviation, and German biotech company Evotec – have cited a lack of accounting staff as a factor for weaknesses in their respective internal controls over financial statement reporting.[23]

He also noted that the reusable plastic container maker, Tupperware, reported it was delaying the filing of its annual report, due to internal control issues and difficulty in hiring enough accountants.[24]

CFO as Scapegoat?

According to a more recent *WSJ* article by Maurer, the accountant shortage has taken on a new dimension: the scapegoating of the CFO, which may provide an even more powerful incentive for CFOs to embrace Gen AI.

---

[22] "The Accountant Shortage Is Showing Up in Financial Statements," WSJ CIO Journal, Mark Maurer, July 11, 2023, https://www.wsj.com/articles/tupperware-delays-filing-annual-results-amid-accountant-shortage-3f4531a0

[23] Ibid

[24] "Tupperware Delays Filing Annual Results Amid Accountant Shortage," WSJ CIO Journal, Mark Maurer and Ben Glickman, March 29, 2024 https://www.wsj.com/articles/tupperware-delays-filing-annual-results-amid-accountant-shortage-3f4531a0

Maurer cited a report from Hudson Labs, an investment research software company, which found that of the over 600 US-listed companies cited insufficient accounting personnel for a material weakness during a 12-month period through June, nearly 30% of them had replaced the CFO within a year's time.[25]

Given Gen AI's ability to access, format, and present financial data in near real time, accounting firms and corporate finance departments may have to overcome risk aversions to new tech adoption.

A key use case emerging in accounting is the automating accruals, one of the most tedious, labor-intensive, and error-prone processes accountants perform. Gen AI can be prompted to automatically identify transactions that require accruals, calculate amounts, and log them in the accounting system, reducing manual workload and minimizing the risk of errors.[26]

For financial staff who produce flash reports and other managerial accounting forms, the new data analysis features of products such as Open AI's ChatGPT-4 Advanced Data Analysis or Microsoft's Fabric are quite compelling. In a matter of seconds (what used to take hours and even days), users can create simple prompts to create datasets, clean and format data, create charts/visualizations, and descriptive statistics. For example, one can upload an income statement and prompt "here's an excel of my startup's finances, make it a dashboard"; test their financial assumptions with "add sensitivity analysis of key assumptions" and/or "run them as a Monte Carlo simulation" and then ask, "assuming a normal distribution, what are outcomes?"[27]

---

[25] Not Enough Accountants? The CFO's Tenure Might Get a Little Shakier, Mark Maurer, WSJ, August 2, 2024, https://www.wsj.com/articles/not-enough-accountants-the-cfos-tenure-might-get-a-little-shakier-9085c9cd

[26] Top Use Cases for Generative AI-Powered Automation, Automation Anywhere, March 29, 2024 https://www.automationanywhere.com/company/blog/automation-ai/top-use-cases-generative-ai-powered-automation

[27] "Improvements to data analysis in ChatGPT. OpenAI, May 16, 2024, https://openai.com/index/improvements-to-data-analysis-in-chatgpt/

Transforming the Organization

As VP, Delivery Management, Broadridge Financial, Iftekhar Alam has a front-row seat to the transformative potential of Gen AI. The firm has created a new organization in the Global Engineering function to focus on applying AI to the firm's next-gen technology products and services.

Leveraging its power to pull together and analyze data from many disparate forms and sources at the presentation layer, Broadridge has created a customized version of a popular chatbot to access, retrieve, summarize, and analyze data at the display, or presentation layer, which means it bypasses the cost and difficulty of centralizing and normalizing information at the deeper data level in massive data warehouses.

This newfound ability is helping the firm to transform from a hosting provider of regulatory disclosure information for publicly held companies to a solutions provider of aggregated data and analytics to financial services firms. These new tools are able to instantly retrieve and aggregate vital financial data from the different business units of a corporation (for corporate finance firms) or the many different holdings of a high net worth individual (for wealth management firms) to create unique and holistic information and analytics about current and prospective clients.

As the former head of Service Delivery and DevOps for the firm, Alam appreciates the challenges of organizational culture change. He sees plenty of evidence to partner with clients across Capital Markets, Wealth, and Asset Management, to accelerate the digital transformation. "It's a huge culture change for us," he notes. "We're quickly changing from a data processing firm to an analytics Fin-Tech company. We're becoming more agile; more involved in innovation, experimentation and prototyping to modernize platforms, digitize communications, and offer next-gen technology and data solutions that help our clients capitalize on emerging opportunities."

AI: "Gateway Drug" to Data Management

As many data managers will confess, most organizations store and archive data the way hoarders keep piles of old newspapers – in the (highly) remote chance the information may be useful at some point in the future. And as we explained in the chapter on Data Governance, all too few organizations have the will, resources, or incentive to make data management a top priority.

George Lawton, London-based American journalist who has written about computers, communications, knowledge management, and business for over 30 years, sees Gen AI as a "gateway drug" for organizations to get their data management act together.

Lawton cites a survey by Everest Group in collaboration with Yates Ltd of more than 50 CIOs that found that executives are ready to move ahead from proof of concepts to full scale implementations of generative AI.[28] The survey reports that nearly 83% of global enterprises are either actively testing their capabilities through pilot programs or have already adopted gen AI for one or more production-grade use cases.

As a possible explanation for this trend, Lawton notes, "Gen AI is sexy, but data management is not."

We would add that data management is not only not sexy, it is incredibly difficult – if it were easier it wouldn't be such a universal problem for most organizations. It typically requires a substantial investment in people, process, and systems; it requires cooperation and coordination among and across functions that often have competing interests and – let's be honest here – it can be incredibly tedious.

---

[28] "Capturing the Generative AI Pulse," Viewpoint, 22 Dec 2023, by Abhishek Singh, Vishal Gupta, Priya Bhalla, https://www2.everestgrp.com/reportaction/ EGR-2023-71-V-6249/Marketing

But there are now signs of other power incentives for organizations to start treating data as a strategic asset: the opportunity to sell their internal data to AI firms.

Hidden Value of Data

Making the data a profit center in its own right solves at least one aspect of the data governance challenge.

Daniel Goldberg, a data executive and industry veteran, foresees an increasing trend in organizations' productizing and monetizing their data to feed the insatiable demand for proprietary data – information beyond the text, visuals, and videos that can be harvested from the Internet – from AI companies to feed their LLMs.

As we've discussed, the lines of business – despite the unrelenting pressure to make their revenue and profit numbers by speeding put processes, squeezing out costs, and offering new product or service features – may have the financial wherewithal to make such investments in data quality and governance, but don't have the authority to transfer budget across departments – even if they wanted to.

Goldberg, who focuses on the financial services sector, suggests that many start-up data providers of "alternative data" (e.g., debit and credit card transaction data, mobile phone foot traffic data, or social media sentiment data) to Wall Street – a term used to describe data not available from traditional sources (financial statements, SEC filings, management presentations, press releases) used by analysts, portfolio managers, traders, and investment bankers — will be beneficiaries.

Go Ask the Bot

Professor Paul Hill at Utah State University has discovered that, in addition to serving as an extremely efficient research assistant and brainstorming partner, ChatGPT has proved to be a great time-saver in responding to common and frequent questions from staff on various departmental policies – for example, on allowable travel expenditures and purchase orders.

Instead of having to explain these (sometimes tacit or not well socialized) advice to inquiring staff, Professor Hill uploaded these departmental rules with his personal instructions in custom GPTs, a feature provided by the Enterprise and Pro versions of ChatGPT, training them to provide accurate responses for employees as to what types of purchases and/or travel arrangement are permissible.

CHAPTER 5

The Intelligent Organization of the Future

(…and the dirty little secret about Gen AI roles)

It's difficult to make predictions, especially about the future.

—Yogi Berra, baseball legend and accidental philosopher

In this chapter, we discuss the near-future transformation of organizational roles and functions.

But we first need to confess the dirty little secret about Gen AI roles.

The Dirty Little Secret

The dirty little secret about Gen AI roles, at least from an organizational point of view, is that they are NOT primarily an IT function – meaning that, not unlike data scientists, Gen AI specialists don't necessarily belong in the IT department.

© Arthur J. O'Connor 2024
A. J. O'Connor, *Organizing for Generative AI and the Productivity Revolution*,
https://doi.org/10.1007/979-8-8688-0959-0_5

Yes, we acknowledge that the skill sets – programming, data engineering and management, model design, testing, validation, and implementation – sounds very techy. And they are – for the most part – at least until low-code and no-code prompting gets so much better (which it appears to be).

But Gen AI is not fundamentally about the care and feeding of an organization's computing infrastructure, nor even developing and implementing new software to support current business processes. It's really about creating entirely new and different ways of doing things – new ways which may, or may not, be supported by IT management or the status quo.

So let us begin our discussion of why major organizational changes could be in play for the corporate IT function and the future design of what might be called "The Intelligent Organization."

Paradigm Shift: From Humans Learning Computers to Computers Learning to Be Human

Information technology has often been called "the backbone of businesses" but in most organizations continues to operate as a stand-alone support function, reporting outside the lines of business.

Recall that the reason for the existence of IT roles and functions arose from the need for **humans** to use and interact with **computers** – hence the distinct disciplines of user interface experience/design, application programming, and computer architecture – at a time when most large organizations owned and maintained their own (on-premises or "on-prem") computing infrastructures.

The Gen AI revolution (and the whole field of Natural Language Processing that preceded it) turns all of that around.

This new wave is about designing and training **computers** to interact with **humans** – to understand the constructs of human language, spelling, grammar, and context constructs (via pre-training) and to generate responses that are accurate and relevant (at least most of the time, via training and fine-tuning) and express those responses in a human-like, socially responsible, and non-offensive manner (via alignment) – that are run by big tech firms and housed in billion-dollar server farms that are remotely accessed via the cloud.

As a result of this paradigm shift, we postulate three trends that will transform roles and functions as well as structures in many organizations.

Trend #1: Migration of Solution Development to Business Units

In a recent survey of CEOs by PWC, 56% identified technological change as the primary reason for their respective strategic initiatives over the next three years.[1] And yet organizationally, we envision that those "strategic initiatives" will perhaps have the greatest impact on the traditional IT department silos that operate outside the other parts of the enterprise.

As we've seen with end-user computing and now "Shadow AI," IT departments find themselves in the near-impossible task in keeping up with end-user experimentation and adoption of Gen AI, which continually outpaces IT's ability to control for security and regulatory compliance risks.

As a practical matter, the sheer enormity of this governance challenge – especially regarding grounding AI with relevant data sources, reference materials, and background context to minimize hallucinations and ensure accurate outputs – IT solution development will need to be closer, and accountable to, profit centers for these risks to be effectively managed.

---

[1] PwC's 27th Annual Global CEO Survey, Thriving in an age of continuous reinvention, https://www.pwc.com/gx/en/issues/c-suite-insights/ceo-survey.html

Current State: IT As Independent "Business Partner"

By way of background, the typical IT organizational structure of most large and even mid-sized corporations is as follows: IT functions as the owner/ manager of the data, communications, and computing infrastructure: management, procurement, data engineering, security, network and systems administration, telecommunications, systems analysis and architecture, and service and support desks.

But from a strategic business perspective, IT's most important function is improving business operations, making processes faster, cheaper, better, as well as enabling new business models and strategies. That is, in addition to being responsible for the security and availability of the enabling software, hardware, and data communications, IT partners with business units to create new processes by procuring, designing, producing, and implementing new functionalities.

Bridging these two worlds (working between IT and the lines of business) are relationship managers (a function that sometimes goes by "Developer Relations," as if programmers were some type of foreign diplomatic corps), who work with product managers, program managers, project managers, and subject matter experts (also known as domain experts) to design, develop, launch, and support new functionalities.

In the age of intelligent machines, we imagine that the lines of business will subsume many of these development functions, as no-code or low-code tools enable even junior business analysts to create innovative applications. As a result, we envision profound changes in the roles of IT staff, who will increasingly be deployed in the lines of business and report directly to the business head.

In this new structure, businesses will be responsible for developing, owning, and managing new enabling technology, and as a result many traditional IT functions will be subsumed into the business units, reporting to business heads. "Business people" (business analysts, salespeople, administrative staff – along with a cadre of data scientists, data engineers, and data analysts and Gen AI specialists embedded in the business unit) will write and run their own code, create, support, and manage their own applications.

We envision the profile and nature of the Gen AI power user to be similar to any professional – people who learn the underlying technologies, master many of the techniques ("the tools of the trade"), stay abreast of important new developments, and develop the experience and wisdom to understand the trade-offs in order to know what best to do, with what types of use cases, in what situation, at what cost.

Moreover, we foresee a new generation of key players – for details on job descriptions and requirements, see **Appendix B: 12 Key Roles** – who take on more strategic, mission-critical roles – tasked with (safely and securely) empowering employees and enabling the enterprise to accelerate innovation, increasingly automate higher-level (knowledge-worker-level) tasks, enhance customer interactions, and super-optimize supply chains to gain competitive advantage and create value.

Trend #2: Acceleration of Infrastructure Outsourcing and Transformation of Corporate IT

In addition to solution development and data science functions migrating to business units, we foresee an acceleration of outsourcing of computing environments to cloud and/or managed services providers.

While the cost of computing continues to decline, the massive investment required to build and maintain data centers capable of manipulating petabytes of data instantaneously required for Gen AI means that most organizations will rent – not own – their computing environments.

For data center engineers and system administrators, especially those at mid-sized firms, the bad news is that, with but a few exceptions, the traditional data center, network control, and system administration functions will transform into a strategic outsourcing function, where the primary functions of the care and feeding of the computing infrastructure will be performed by cloud and third-party providers and managed via the terms and conditions of vendor contractors and service level agreements.

This trend is prompting advisory firms to build out their networks of technology partners to give their managed services clients access to the tech they need plus the skills to deploy it. The management of computing environments will fall to managed services outsourcing and procurement functions, much as telecommunications and data communications services have over recent decades.

And there's also the challenge of recruiting the right talent to keep pace with AI, which is why the big professional services firms are becoming full-service managed service vendors.[2] There's nothing new about managed services and organizations migrating their computing environments to the cloud – what's new is that the design, management, and upkeep of massive, complex server farms required for Gen AI greatly exceed the financial resources of all but the largest organizations.

With the expanded offerings of advanced models through managed services that are accessible through just about any device and code bots that can be easily instructed to retrieve and clean data from various external and internal data stores, as well as write code to interrogate the data and produce results, the role of the IT department as the sole, legitimate producer of technology is changing fast.

If current trends in outsourcing and subscription services continue, it may well be that the balance of the IT organization will evolve into a higher level, flatter organization that develops and implements architectural and technical standards, policies, and procedures, along with performing an "R&D" or "think tank" function – constantly surveying the AI ecosystem for new capabilities to pitch to the business heads and senior staff.

---

[2] "The role of consultants is changing as the rise of managed services turns them from advisors into service providers," Fortune, Ian McConnell, July 3, 2024.

Trend #3: Upsetting the Power Hierarchy and the Great Rotation

The democratization of expertise may also have some interesting implications on leveling the playing field and even upsetting the power hierarchy in many organizations.

A research study from the Stanford Business Graduate School of over 5,000 customer support employees at a Fortune 500 software firm found that those employees using a generative AI tool increased not only worker productivity but also customer satisfaction and employee retention.[3]

But perhaps most interesting was this finding: while the average increase in handling calls and resolving issues was 14% for these AI-assisted users, the gain in productivity was greatest for the least experienced workers, who saw productivity gains of up to 35%.[4]

Enabling the junior employees to perform as seasoned professions may have some powerful implications in job requirements, compensation levels, and reporting hierarchies.

And then there's the phenomenon of what might be called "the great rotation of the employee base."

As we discussed in Chapter 1, history shows that productivity revolutions change – not eliminate – the number and nature of jobs. And we also touched upon the Frontier of Automation, which states that there's a point where the complexity of tasks that machines are capable of performing will eventually match and surpass those of humans.

---

[3] "Generative AI at Work," Stanford Business Graduate School, Erik Brynjolfsson, Danielle Li, Lindsey R. Raymond, November 2023 https://www.gsb.stanford.edu/faculty-research/working-papers/generative-ai-work
[4] Ibid

So while it's wonderful that these tools enable us to work at higher-level tasks, the sad truth is that not all of us are willing or capable of higher-level functions. Despite all the talk of upskilling and AI readiness, we all have different levels of cognitive and creative abilities – our own intersections with the Frontier of Automation.

Industry 4.0 may result in a major change in the mix of employee skill sets, in which more creative, tech-savvy (possibly younger, more educated?) workers become a larger percentage of the employee base, supplanting those who transition to a smaller number of more labor-intensive, high-touch, personal service-oriented (and less compensated?) roles.

In some ways, this trend would represent a continuation (and possible acceleration) of income equality in the past several decades, largely attributed to globalization and the productivity-boosting effects of the digital revolution. The skewed benefits of these trends favored professionals and college-educated white-collar workers – so-called knowledge workers – at the expense of semi-skilled labor.

This observation is consistent with findings by economists at MIT and Boston, who attributed somewhere between half and a majority (up to 70%) of changes in US wages from 1980 to 2016 by relative wage decline for workers who performed routine tasks in industries experiencing rapid automation.[5]

It should be noted that another MIT economist offers a contrarian assessment of the impact of AI on the workforce, by which the democratization of expertise levels the playing field for all. As its author, David Autor, puts it: "The unique opportunity that AI offers humanity is to push back against the process started by computerization — to extend the relevance, reach and value of human expertise to a larger set of workers."[6]

---

[5] "Tasks, Automation, and the Rise in U.S. Wage Inequality," Daron Acemoglu, Pascual Restrepo, Econometrica, Vol. 90, No. 5, September, 2022 https://doi.org/10.3982/ECTA19815

[6] "AI Could Actually Help Rebuild The Middle Class," David Autor, Noema Magazine, February12, 2024 https://www.noemamag.com/how-ai-could-help-rebuild-the-middle-class/

For now, we'll leave that debate to the futurists. But before we leave this chapter, let's touch upon two emerging trends in organizational functions: "AutoML" and, coming soon, "LLM Ops."

"AutoML"

Perhaps the most important recent developments in Gen AI have been automated machine learning (AutoML), specialized code bots, and prompt programming frameworks such as Declarative Self-Improving Language Programs (DSPy) for automating much of the process of creating prompts, intelligent agents, and self-optimizing/self-learning data pipelines.

Until recently, virtually every step in the current prototypical data science pipeline, such as data preprocessing, feature engineering, and hyper-parameter optimization, has to be done manually by machine learning experts. Regardless of whether you're building classifiers or training regressions, this manually intensive process can be thought of as a generalized search concept, requiring specialized search algorithms for finding the optimal solutions for each component piece of the ML pipeline.

AutoML changes all that, enabling an automated, faster, streamlined development process by which a few lines of code can generate the code necessary to begin developing a machine learning model to provide explainable and reproducible results. These state-of-the-art tools can streamline complex processes such as data cleaning, model building, interpretation, and report writing.

As a result, they reshape the role of data scientists. We argue that LLMs are transforming the responsibilities of data scientists, shifting their focus from hands-on coding, data-wrangling, and conducting standard analyses to assessing and managing analyses performed by these automated AIs.

This evolution of roles is reminiscent of the transition from a software engineer to a product manager, where strategic planning, coordinating resources, and overseeing the overall product life cycle supersede the task of writing code.

Importantly, AutoML allows for greater access to AI development for those without the theoretical background currently needed for specialized knowledge in data science. With the advent of AutoML, the role of the data scientist is shifting from model building to data understanding and feature engineering. The successful data scientist of the future will need to be a good communicator, have strong business acumen, and be able to work closely with cross-functional teams, while cultivating diverse skill sets such as LLM-informed creativity, critical thinking, AI-guided programming, and interdisciplinary knowledge.

Coming Soon: "LLM Ops"

LLM Ops (Large Language Model Operations) will significantly impact the organizational roles and structure of typical corporate IT functions. This emerging field focuses on the operational aspects of deploying, managing, and maintaining large language models in production environments.

The introduction of LLM Ops will necessitate new specialized roles within IT departments:

1. LLM Engineers: These professionals will focus on deploying, scaling, and optimizing large language models for specific business use cases. They'll need to understand both the technical aspects of LLMs and the business contexts in which they're applied.

2. Prompt Engineers: As prompt engineering becomes crucial for effective LLM use, dedicated roles may emerge to design, test, and refine prompts for various applications across the organization.

3. LLM Performance Analysts: These specialists will monitor and analyze LLM performance, identifying areas for improvement and ensuring models meet business requirements.

4. AI Ethicists: With the increased use of LLMs, organizations may need dedicated professionals to address ethical concerns, bias, and fairness in AI outputs.

…as well as the evolution and expansion of current roles:

1. DevOps Engineers: They'll need to expand their skills to include LLM deployment and management, potentially evolving into "AI Ops" specialists.

2. Data Engineers: Their role will expand to include preparing and managing data specifically for LLM training and fine-tuning.

3. Security Specialists: They'll need to develop expertise in AI-specific security concerns, such as prompt injection attacks and data privacy in LLM contexts.

4. IT Architects: They'll need to design systems that can effectively integrate LLMs into existing IT infrastructure.

We also envision that LLM Ops may lead to structural changes in IT departments:

1. AI/LLM Centers of Excellence: Organizations may create centralized teams dedicated to LLM Ops, serving as internal consultants and setting best practices.

2. Cross-functional Teams: IT may form more cross-functional teams that include LLM specialists, domain experts, and business analysts to tackle specific LLM projects.

3. Flatter Hierarchies: The need for rapid innovation and adaptation in LLM Ops may lead to flatter organizational structures that allow for quicker decision-making and implementation.

4. Embedded LLM Specialists: Some organizations may choose to embed LLM specialists within different business units rather than centralizing all LLM expertise in IT.

LLM Ops will necessitate new processes within IT:

1. LLM Lifecycle Management: IT will need to establish processes for the entire lifecycle of LLMs, from selection and customization to deployment, monitoring, and retirement.

2. Continuous Learning and Adaptation: Given the rapid pace of LLM advancements, IT will need to implement processes for continuous learning and quick adoption of new techniques.

3. LLM Governance: IT will need to develop governance frameworks specific to LLM use, ensuring compliance, security, and ethical use across the organization.

4. Collaborative Development: IT may need to implement new workflows that allow for closer collaboration between LLM specialists and business users in developing and refining LLM applications.

To support LLM Ops, IT departments will need to focus on skill development:

1. Internal Training Programs: IT may need to develop comprehensive training programs to upskill existing staff in LLM-related technologies and best practices.

2. External Partnerships: Organizations may form partnerships with academic institutions or AI companies to ensure their IT staff stays current with the latest LLM developments.

3. Continuous Learning Culture: IT departments will need to foster a culture of continuous learning to keep pace with the rapidly evolving field of LLM Ops.

In conclusion, LLM Ops will drive significant changes in the organizational roles and structure of corporate IT functions. It will require the creation of new specialized roles, the evolution of existing ones, and potentially new organizational structures to effectively manage and leverage LLMs. IT departments will need to adapt quickly, developing new processes and focusing on continuous skill development to meet the challenges and opportunities presented by LLM Ops.

We next turn to the topic of changing demands of organizational leadership in the age of intelligent machines.

CHAPTER 6

Leadership in the Intelligent Organization

You get more with a kind word and a gun than with a kind word alone.

—Al Capone, gangster

At the start, we stated that this book is ultimately a leadership guide, a handbook to help executives build the right capabilities with the right teams to succeed.

Despite all the hype about the potential and risks of generative AI, the key question remains: how do leaders effectively **manage** the democratization of expertise and production? To draw an analogy from the industrial age, how do you manage the production line when everyone can produce their own finished product?

How do leaders manage and coordinate all this independently generated output for the collective good of the enterprise?

© Arthur J. O'Connor 2024
A. J. O'Connor, *Organizing for Generative AI and the Productivity Revolution*,
https://doi.org/10.1007/979-8-8688-0959-0_6

And make no mistake: there **is** a dire need for strong leadership and clear controls. In the Introduction, we described the current environment as "Wally World" – the lack of bright lines in regulatory guidelines or industry standards.

And there's mounting evidence that the risks of "Shadow AI" are really starting to get out of control.

A recent survey by Microsoft and LinkedIn of 31,000 working adults reported that 75% of knowledge workers said they had started using AI on the job.[1] But most (78%) of them said that they are bringing their own AI tools to work, and only 39% reported their employers had supplied them with AI training.[2]

Yikes!

Even at this early stage of the Productivity Revolution, it's becoming more clear that there are certain tasks that the current generation of Gen AI outperforms humans; but other areas where it fails miserably. Leadership in the era of human-machine collaboration or "co-intelligence" will require rethinking and reengineering processes and tasks where Gen AI excels at improving human performance, while balancing the opportunities relative to risks.

This chapter goes into more detail about the changing nature of organizational leadership in this new age of intelligent machines.

---

[1] 2024 Work Trend Index Annual Report, Microsoft and LinkedIn, https://www.microsoft.com/en-us/worklab/work-trend-index/ai-at-work-is-here-now-comes-the-hard-part

[2] Ibid

Demise of Command and Control Micromanagement

If there's one key takeaway message from this chapter is that, with all due respect to Mr. Capone, the coercive, tried-but-not-always-true, command and control or "Theory X"[3] style of management – long the favorite among micromanagers – will most likely not survive in the era of human-AI collaboration.

The Productivity Revolution requires deep collaboration and alignment across functions, requiring both a top-down as well as bottom-up approach. Truth is, much of the real innovation in infusing Gen AI into mission-critical applications will come from individual contributors experimenting with new techniques and model variants, which places even greater emphasis on collaborative leadership, with greater numbers of key decision-makers in the power hierarchy.

Again, the history of the growth of the new roles in the C-suite from the previous digital revolution reveals the origins of this trend.

Expansion of Leadership Roles

Up until the late 1970s, at the dawn of the digital revolution, the head honcho in the corporate hierarchy was the President or Chief Executive Officer, to whom reported a Chief Financial Officer, Chief Operating Officer, a General Counsel, and maybe a Chief Administrative Officer. That's about it. The director of IT, if there was one, most likely reported to the CFO or COO.

---

[3] "Theory X and Theory Y," Wikipedia, https://en.wikipedia.org/wiki/Theory_X_and_Theory_Y

Today, the typical corporate IT organization looks very different: there's a Chief Information Officer, a Chief Technology Officer, and in many organizations, a Chief Data Officer, and even a Chief Transformation or Chief Change Management Officer – and coming soon, a Chief AI Officer.

This book propounds that exponential growth of AI will usher in not just technological disruption but a fundamental reimagining of organizational leadership. It will call for leaders who are as adept at understanding algorithms as they are at inspiring people, who can navigate complexity with humility, and who see diversity not as a box to be checked but as a dynamic force driving innovation and resilience.

In this new paradigm, the archetypal leader evolves from a commanding general to an orchestral conductor—less focused on issuing orders and more on harmonizing the unique talents of each individual, human and AI alike. The organizations that thrive will be those that broaden their conception of leadership, valuing a tapestry of skills, backgrounds, and perspectives.

As we stand on the cusp of this AI-driven transformation, one thing becomes clear: the future belongs not to the loudest voice in the room, but to the one that can bring forth a chorus of voices, united in purpose, diverse in thought, and empowered by technology.

As Tech Skills Become More Critical, so Do Soft Skills

According to *The Wall Street Journal*, "More CIOs are reporting directly to their chief executives, a reflection of the role's increased importance in helping set corporate AI strategies to keep up with the competition."[4]

---

[4] "AI Puts CIOs in the Spotlight, Right Next to the CEO," Belle Lin, WSJ, June 12, 2024 https://www.wsj.com/articles/ai-puts-cios-in-the-spotlight-alongside-the-ceo-efa2f9d2?mod=latest_headlines

But one of the great ironies in the Productivity Revolution may be that, as tech skills become more valued by CEOs, the Gen AI revolution may pose an even greater need for soft skills. We hypothesize at least two main reasons for this.

One is simply a function of operating leverage. As power users of AI become more and more productive and contribute more to organizational competitive advantage and value creation, the more critical the leadership and management of those individual contributors and team members become.

Just imagine the oversight and coordination challenge when a manager's team of 10 people now can produce the output of 100 people in the same amount of time! As individual contributors become more empowered and productive, leadership competencies will require higher degrees of emotional and social intelligence – as well as technical competencies – to motivate and manage these individuals for the collective good and ensure compliance with sound business practices and policies.

The second reason relates to how the unprecedented rate of change that the exponential growth of AI will impact organizations. As we've noted, organizational roles and hierarchical power structures are typically slow to adapt to technological change, due to the phenomenon known as "organizational inertia." The ability to effectively lead organizational change management may take on greater significance, which means that cross-disciplinary matrix management skills (aka "herding the cats") will take on new dimensions.

So, as strange as it may seem, it may be that creativity, empathy, critical thinking, and adaptability become the most important leadership skills in the era of intelligent machines.

The Paradox of Empowerment: Why Leadership Matters More Than Ever

As organizations increasingly adopt generative AI, the nature of work is undergoing a profound transformation. Individual contributors and team members, armed with these powerful tools, are becoming extraordinarily productive, contributing more significantly to their organizations' competitive advantage and value creation. This shift is not just a matter of increased output; it represents a fundamental change in the dynamics of how work is done and how organizations function. In this new landscape, the role of leadership takes on even greater importance, albeit in ways that might not be immediately obvious.

At first glance, it might seem that highly capable individuals, augmented by AI, would require less oversight and management. However, the opposite is true. As individual contributors become more empowered, the need for effective leadership intensifies. This paradox arises from several factors.

Alignment and Purpose

With great individual power comes the risk of divergence. Each team member, highly productive in their own right, may pursue objectives that, while valuable, do not necessarily align with the organization's overall goals. Leaders must therefore excel at articulating a compelling vision and fostering a shared sense of purpose that transcends individual achievements.

The Human Element

Despite the capabilities of AI, uniquely human qualities – creativity, empathy, ethical judgment, and complex problem-solving – remain irreplaceable. Leaders play a crucial role in championing these aspects, ensuring that AI augments rather than replaces human potential.

Navigating Complexity

AI-driven environments are characterized by rapid change and high complexity. Individuals, no matter how skilled, can easily become overwhelmed or lose sight of the bigger picture. Leadership provides the necessary perspective and stability, helping teams navigate uncertainty.

Employee Morale and Engagement

By some accounts, leadership in the organizational adoption of Gen AI is mostly about cheerleading; the role of the CEO is to evangelize its tremendous productivity benefits. This enthusiasm and energy then cascades down to the rank file, turbocharging business value.

We beg to disagree. We acknowledge the potential for Gen AI to improve the quality (not just the productivity) of job experience by enabling employees to assume higher-level and potentially more creative and fulfilling functions – creating the potential for greater job satisfaction – just as previous industrial revolutions have done. However, we also view the media frenzy and constant drum beat of how AI will replace humans as mostly negatively affecting employee morale and engagement, creating great challenges for leaders in cultivating and maintaining a positive organizational culture.

All the more reason that emotional intelligence, or soft skills, becomes all the more critical as a leadership trait.

But before we get into how Gen AI may reshape the nature of organizational leadership, we need to tackle a thorny issue few seem to want to talk about: "the imposter syndrome."

The Dangerous Impact of Imposter Syndrome on Organizational Culture

One of the biggest challenges that some executives face in cultivating AI literacy in their own organizations is that they feel unqualified; they're not knowledgeable enough, not smart enough about the technology.

A recent survey of 10,000 workers and executives by Korn Ferry cited AI as one reason 71% of CEOs and two-thirds of other senior leaders said they had "impostor syndrome" in their positions.[5]

As a leader, this is a fear you must face, a skill set you need to develop – and a condition you can't afford to have.

As you already know, culture is a reflection of leadership. And when a leader pretends, it signals to everyone in the organization that it's okay to pretend – creating a dangerous mindset that it's okay to pretend to know things that they don't bother to learn or master.

Yes, we acknowledge that it's easy to be intimidated by all the jargon. You may sometimes fear that what you've heard – that the half-life of skills, or the amount of time a given skill is useful, is shrinking – and thus you're on the verge of becoming obsolete. You may have even come to believe that the real problem is that you don't even know **what** to learn.

We encourage leaders to be transparent about the levels of their AI skills and knowledge, to bone up on the basics, and to create a culture of continuous learning – for everyone in their respective organization.

And let us reiterate what we've said before: unless you're a major Brainiac, there's literally no way you can keep up with all the major advances and new developments in Intelligent Systems – much less keep on top of all the hype from social media, the financial press, and Wall Street.

---

[5] "No One Wants to Sound Clueless About AI. Especially Your Boss," WSJ, R. Smith, June 24, 2024, `https://www.wsj.com/lifestyle/workplace/still-trying-to-sound-smart-about-ai-the-boss-is-too-fc33dd80?st=`

We advocate that you don't need to be a "digital sherpa" to lead. Instead, we urge leaders to focus on the gist of what these new technologies make possible and build strong teams with the right mandates and robust development processes to ensure that the solutions fit your business strategies and use cases while ensuring the data are of high quality, the risks managed, the outcomes tested, and the results measured and validated.

The New Leadership Imperative: Emotional and Social Intelligence

In this context, traditional command-and-control leadership models fall short. The productivity gains offered by AI are easily offset if leadership fails to evolve. The new imperative for leaders is the cultivation of high degrees of emotional and social intelligence.

Understanding and Managing Emotions

Leaders must become astute observers and managers of emotions – both their own and those of their team members. This involves recognizing the emotional currents that underlie AI-augmented work, from the excitement of breakthroughs to the frustration of setbacks, and guiding these energies constructively.

Building Genuine Connections

In a world where technical tasks are increasingly automated, human connections become a primary driver of engagement and loyalty. Leaders need to invest time and effort in understanding the aspirations, fears, and motivations of each team member, fostering an environment of trust and mutual respect.

Facilitating Collaboration

AI may boost individual productivity, but organizational success still hinges on effective collaboration. Leaders must become skilled facilitators, bringing diverse perspectives together, managing conflicts, and nurturing an environment where the whole truly becomes greater than the sum of its parts.

Cultivating Psychological Safety

Innovation in AI-driven environments requires experimentation and, inevitably, some failures. Leaders must foster psychological safety, where team members feel secure in taking risks, sharing unconventional ideas, and learning from mistakes. This involves modeling vulnerability, admitting one's own errors, and treating failures as valuable learning opportunities.

Personalizing Motivation

With AI handling many routine tasks, work becomes more personalized. Leaders need to understand what drives each individual – be it autonomy, mastery, purpose, or other factors – and tailor their approach accordingly. One-size-fits-all incentive structures give way to individualized growth plans and recognition systems.

Championing Ethical AI Use

The power of generative AI brings with it significant ethical responsibilities. Leaders must not only establish clear guidelines for responsible AI use but also embody ethical principles in their own decisions and actions. They become the moral compass, helping their teams navigate the complex terrain of AI ethics.

Continuous Learning and Adaptability

In the face of AI's rapid evolution, leaders can no longer rely solely on accumulated experience. They must become lifelong learners, constantly updating their understanding of technological advancements and their implications. Moreover, they need to instill this spirit of continuous learning throughout their teams.

Balancing AI and Human Contributions

Perhaps the most nuanced aspect of leadership in this new era is orchestrating the interplay between AI and human strengths. Leaders must develop a deep understanding of both, knowing when to leverage AI for efficiency and scale and when to prioritize human insight and creativity.

The Velocity of Change: Leading in an Era of AI-Driven Exponential Growth

You might be asking yourself: how the rapid growth of AI will impact organizations, the challenges of change management, and the potential shifts in leadership demographics and traits?

The advent of generative AI marks not just another step in technological evolution, but a leap into a new paradigm characterized by unprecedented rates of change. This exponential growth challenges traditional notions of organizational adaptability and strategic planning. Leaders find themselves navigating a landscape where the horizon itself seems to be accelerating away from them.

The Shortening Half-Life of Knowledge

In this new era, the shelf-life of skills and knowledge diminishes rapidly. What was cutting-edge yesterday becomes obsolete today. Organizations can no longer rely on static competencies or fixed strategic plans. Instead, they must cultivate dynamic capabilities – the ability to continuously reconfigure resources, processes, and strategies in response to shifting technological landscapes.

From Forecasting to Scenario Planning

Traditional forecasting methods, based on extrapolating past trends, prove inadequate in the face of AI's nonlinear growth. Executives must shift toward robust scenario planning, envisioning multiple possible futures and preparing their organizations for agility rather than predictability.

The Imperative of Organizational Ambidexterity

Leaders are challenged to simultaneously manage today's business while building tomorrow's. This ambidexterity – exploiting current capabilities while exploring new opportunities – becomes not just a desirable trait but a survival imperative in the AI age.

Change Management Redefined: From Episodes to Continuous Transformation

In a world where AI capabilities double in fractions of the time of previous technological advances, change is no longer an episodic event but a constant state. This reality demands a fundamental rethinking of change management strategies.

Embedding Change Resilience

Rather than managing discrete change initiatives, leaders must focus on building change resilience into the very DNA of their organizations. This involves fostering a culture where adaptability is the norm, where employees at all levels are empowered to initiate and drive change.

Decentralized Change Leadership

The pace of AI-driven change outstrips the capacity of centralized, top-down change management. Executives need to distribute change leadership throughout the organization, equipping teams with the autonomy and resources to respond rapidly to emerging opportunities and challenges.

Continuous Listening and Dialogue

In this fluid environment, annual surveys and periodic town halls are insufficient. Leaders must establish ongoing, multi-directional communication channels. Real-time feedback loops, leveraging AI-driven analytics, allow for the rapid sensing of employee sentiments, concerns, and ideas, enabling responsive and inclusive change strategies.

Learning As a Strategic Priority

With the half-life of skills shrinking, learning becomes a core strategic function. Leaders must champion a shift from episodic training to continuous, personalized learning journeys for every employee. Learning itself needs to be about learning how to learn, adapting to new information and circumstances swiftly.

The Changing Face of Leadership: Diversity As a Competitive Advantage

The exponential growth of AI not only accelerates change but also reshapes the qualities required for effective leadership. This shift has profound implications for the demographic composition of leadership teams, potentially altering the current mix of gender and race among CEOs.

From Command to Collaboration

Historically, traits such as assertiveness, competitiveness, and risk-taking – often stereotypically associated with male leadership – were prized. However, in an AI-augmented world, where machines increasingly handle analytical and routine decision-making tasks, uniquely human qualities come to the fore. Emotional intelligence, empathy, and the ability to foster collaboration become critical success factors.

The Inclusivity Imperative

As organizations grapple with complex, multifaceted challenges, diverse perspectives become invaluable. Leaders who can create inclusive environments, where a wide range of voices are heard and valued, gain a decisive edge. This shift favors those with high social intelligence and cultural competence – traits that cut across gender and racial lines but have often been undervalued in traditional corporate settings.

Redefining Strength

In this new landscape, strength is redefined. It's less about individual heroics and more about the capacity to build and nurture high-performing teams. It's about vulnerability – admitting what one doesn't know and seeking input from others. It's about emotional courage – having difficult conversations and standing up for ethical principles in the face of AI's powerful capabilities.

The Mentorship Advantage
With the rapid evolution of technology, cross-generational learning becomes crucial. Reverse mentoring programs, where younger employees guide senior leaders on emerging trends, flourish alongside traditional mentorship. Leaders who excel at both teaching and learning, who can bridge generational and technological divides, rise to prominence.

Recruitment, Retention, and Promotion in the AI Era

The shifting demands of leadership in an AI-driven world necessitate a reevaluation of how organizations identify, develop, and retain talent.

Beyond the Resume
Traditional credentials and past performance, while still relevant, become less predictive of future success. Recruitment increasingly focuses on assessing adaptability, learning agility, and relational skills. Innovative approaches, such as AI-enabled simulations and collaborative problem-solving exercises, help identify candidates with the requisite cognitive and emotional dexterity.

Retention Through Growth
In a fast-changing environment, employees stay not for stability but for growth opportunities. Organizations retain top talent by offering personalized development paths, stretch assignments, and the chance to work on meaningful, AI-amplified projects. Leaders who act as coaches, helping their teams navigate this growth, become talent magnets.

Promotion Criteria Evolve
Advancement is no longer solely based on individual achievements but increasingly on one's contribution to team and organizational learning. Those who elevate others, who create psychologically safe spaces for experimentation, and who successfully lead through influence rather than authority, are earmarked for senior roles.

Beware the Tech Mindset

We would be remiss if we didn't mention in this chapter on leadership perhaps one of the most significant challenges facing leaders: the occupational biases of the AI industry itself.

Most people who run LLM companies are researchers and scientists. And they, like most data scientists, can care most about creating the best, most powerful, accurate model.

The job of the organizational leader is to challenge and temper these occupational biases with hard questions as to assessing the benefits, relative to costs.

Again, the challenge is to avoid getting distracted by the tech buzzwords. Remember: it is not about what all the new LLM variants and new techniques developed at Stanford or Open AI can do. It's all about what the tech, at what cost, can do for **your organization** – given your culture, business model, talent pool, organizational structure, and competitive strengths.

Short Term vs. Long Term

Another big challenge for decision-makers and leaders is how best to balance priorities in investing in Gen AI capabilities.

As you already know, the more practical, common-sense approach is to look for the "low-hanging" fruit – opportunities that present the biggest and/or quick benefit at the least amount of cost or difficulty in implementation.

Yet the downside of relying exclusively on this strategy is the criticism of taking a short-term, piecemeal fragmented approach rather than a holistic, strategic approach to AI adoption.

Given the critical role of human judgment, creativity, and oversight in successful AI integration, it's difficult to generalize on the best approach for any given organization.

Successful Gen AI adoption requires continuous learning as AI technologies rapidly evolve, and the vital roles of leadership are to balance between innovation and responsible use of AI by creating a healthy organizational culture of adaptation and transformation.

R&D Goes Mainstream

Lastly, we make one more prediction on how Gen AI will transform the organizational landscape. As AI capabilities grow exponentially, we posit, it will become increasingly important that organizational leaders and their senior management team keep abreast of what AI ecosystem makes possible at what price.

As a result, one consequence that seems reasonable to assume would be that now even mid-sized organizations have an R&D department (or an equivalent of such) – a function once reserved for only the largest companies in a subset of industries – to be on the lookout to identify the application of AI capabilities in high-impact use cases across different departments.

While the upside of Gen AI will impact types of organizations at different rates and scale, it will become increasingly important that the organizational leaders and the senior management keep abreast of developments in their respective space. Some of these organizations may be too small to make investments in Gen AI, but they need to be knowledgeable enough by constantly surveying the AI landscape in order to be able to subscribe to cost-effective offerings that provide them a competitive advantage in identifying and capture market demand, streamlining administrative or internal operations, or optimizing their supply chains.

The Human at the Heart of the AI Revolution

As generative AI reshapes the organizational landscape, making individual contributors more powerful than ever, it paradoxically underscores the irreplaceable value of human-centric leadership. Technical prowess alone is insufficient; it must be complemented by the ability to inspire, unite, and nurture teams.

The successful leaders of tomorrow will not be those who best understand AI, but those who best understand people. They will be distinguished by their capacity to build meaningful relationships, align diverse talents toward common goals, and create environments where both humans and AI can reach their full potential.

In essence, as our tools become more advanced, our need for emotionally intelligent, socially adept leadership becomes more acute. The AI revolution, for all its technological marvels, ultimately reaffirms a timeless truth: at the heart of every great organization are the human connections and shared aspirations that inspire us to achieve the extraordinary.

As we've noted, adopting generative AI brings about significant behavioral changes within organizations, profoundly impacting how employees learn, collaborate, make decisions, and exercise autonomy. From an organizational psychology perspective, one of the most notable changes is an increase in learning agility. Employees must quickly adapt to new tools and methodologies, necessitating a culture that prioritizes continuous learning and development. This shift often involves implementing training programs, workshops, and fostering a mindset oriented toward perpetual growth and skill enhancement.

Generative AI stimulates a culture of experimentation and innovation. By enabling rapid prototyping and trialing of new ideas, organizations encourage employees to feel safe experimenting and failing fast. This atmosphere of innovation, however, requires strong psychological safety and support from leadership to thrive.

The integration of AI enhances collaboration across functions. AI systems often necessitate teamwork among IT, data science, marketing, and operations, promoting an environment where diverse skill sets are valued and utilized. Alongside enhanced collaboration, there is a need for transparency and clear communication about AI's capabilities, limitations, and impact on various roles. Leaders must communicate openly about how AI will be used and its implications for job functions, helping to manage expectations and reduce uncertainty.

Checklist for Leaders

Finally, here's a short checklist for leaders for supporting such desired organizational behaviors.

Provide Strategic Foresight and Prioritize Initiatives

- Set Clear Priorities: Leaders must establish clear priorities that balance the need for speed with safety. This involves identifying critical areas where rapid innovation is necessary while ensuring that robust safety protocols are in place. By prioritizing initiatives based on their potential impact and associated risks, leaders can manage resources effectively and focus on high-value projects without compromising safety.

- Develop a Roadmap: A well-defined roadmap that outlines short-term and long-term goals helps in maintaining this balance. The roadmap should include milestones for innovation while incorporating checkpoints for risk assessment and mitigation. This structured approach allows for agile responses to emerging opportunities and threats.

- Stress Transparency: Clear and transparent communication becomes vital. Leaders must ensure that all stakeholders are informed about the progress of projects, potential risks, and the measures in place to mitigate them. This transparency builds trust and ensures that everyone is aligned with the organization's goals.

Create a Supportive Culture

- Promote a Culture of Agility and Resilience: Leaders play a crucial role in fostering a culture that values both agility and resilience. Encouraging employees to be adaptable and resilient in the face of change ensures that the organization can move quickly when necessary without sacrificing safety. This involves training programs that emphasize flexibility, problem-solving, and proactive risk management.

- Empower Teams: Empowering teams to make decisions at various levels promotes faster execution while maintaining control over safety. Leaders should delegate authority appropriately and ensure that teams have the resources and autonomy to innovate responsibly. This empowerment fosters a sense of ownership and accountability among employees.

Integrate Risk Management with Innovation

- Implement Robust Risk Management Frameworks: As we've noted before, effective risk management frameworks are essential for balancing speed and safety. These frameworks should include regular risk assessments, scenario planning, and contingency plans. By anticipating potential risks and having mitigation strategies in place, organizations can innovate swiftly without exposing themselves to undue dangers.

- Encourage Responsible Innovation: Leaders must promote responsible innovation by setting clear ethical guidelines and ensuring compliance with industry standards and regulations. This includes conducting thorough due diligence on new technologies and practices before implementation and continuously monitoring their impact.

Mitigate Cross-Functional Tensions

- Increase Collaboration and Cross-Functional Teams: The need to balance speed and safety often leads to increased collaboration across departments. Cross-functional teams become more common as they bring together diverse expertise to address complex challenges. This shift encourages a more integrated approach to problem-solving and decision-making.

- Support Evolution of Roles: As organizations navigate these tensions, traditional roles may evolve. For example, risk management roles might expand to include more proactive elements, focusing not just on identifying and mitigating risks but also on fostering innovation in a safe manner. Similarly, innovation roles might incorporate more aspects of risk assessment and management.

Embrace Agility, Learning, and Development

- Accelerate Adoption of Agile Project Management: The adoption of agile project management methodologies becomes more prevalent. Agile practices allow organizations to iterate quickly, respond to changes, and incorporate feedback continuously while maintaining a focus on safety and quality. Roles such as Scrum Masters and Product Owners become integral to facilitating this balance.

- Increase Focus on Learning and Development: Continuous learning and development become even more critical. Employees need to be equipped with the latest knowledge and skills to navigate the fast-paced and ever-changing landscape. This might involve more frequent training sessions, workshops, and access to learning resources.

Conclusion

Navigating the tensions of moving fast and staying safe requires strategic foresight, strong leadership, and a robust risk management framework. Leaders must foster a culture that values agility and resilience, empower teams, and encourage responsible innovation. These behavioral tensions shape changes in organizational roles and functions, leading to increased collaboration, evolving roles, agile project management, and a greater focus on learning and development. By effectively managing these tensions, organizations can innovate swiftly and safely, ensuring sustained growth and success.

In conclusion, the adoption of generative AI leads to profound behavioral changes within organizations. These changes impact learning, collaboration, decision-making, and autonomy. Leaders must balance the drive for innovation with effective risk management by setting a clear vision, engaging stakeholders, fostering an innovative culture, and ensuring ethical AI use. This balanced approach enables organizations to harness the potential of generative AI while safeguarding their brand and minimizing risks.

PART III

What Regulators and Academics Are Saying

CHAPTER 7

Regulation and Compliance

I'm increasingly inclined to think that there should be some regulatory oversight, maybe at the national and international level, just to make sure that we don't do something very foolish. I mean with artificial intelligence we're summoning the demon.[1]

—Elon Musk, tech billionaire

Part III describes how regulators and legislators are influencing the scope of risk management, compliance, and audit functions in organizations implementing Gen AI and reviews some recent academic research on organizational adoption to these new technologies and their impact on the workplace.

In this chapter, we discuss the new roles, functions, standards/practices, and organizational structures firms are creating to comply with lawful and ethical business practices as well as in the expectation of new legislation, regulations, and industry guidelines governing the use of all forms of AI.

---

[1] Elon Musk: "With artificial intelligence we are summoning the demon." Matt McFarland,

Washington Post, October 24, 2014 https://www.washingtonpost.com/news/innovations/wp/2014/10/24/elon-musk-with-artificial-intelligence-we-are-summoning-the-demon/

© Arthur J. O'Connor 2024
A. J. O'Connor, *Organizing for Generative AI and the Productivity Revolution*, https://doi.org/10.1007/979-8-8688-0959-0_7

The following chapter, Chapter 8, covers some of the current academic research on the use of Gen AI in the workplace, in the hopes of shedding some light on how organizations are adapting to this new environment, the potential upside for its application, and some of the potential barriers of broader user adoption.

In the final concluding chapter, we suggest some paths forward on preparing for the next big thing in Gen AI.

The Regulatory Challenge: Anticipating the Dangers

Regulators and lawmakers face the near-impossible challenge of establishing rules and guidelines to protect the public from the potentially tremendous harm from the intentional misuse or unintentional consequences of Gen AI technologies.

As we've noted, there are many issues around the design and use of generative AI, reflecting the technology's rapid advancement and potential impacts across various sectors of society. Here are some of the key concerns.

1. Bias and Discrimination

   Models can inadvertently perpetuate or amplify societal biases present in their training data. This could lead to unfair or discriminatory outcomes in areas like hiring, lending, or criminal justice.

2. Transparency and Interpretability

   Proprietary, or closed, large language models operate as "black boxes," making it difficult for humans to understand how the models calculated their outputs. This lack of transparency poses challenges for accountability and oversight.

116

3. Misinformation and Disinformation

    Regulators worry about generative AI's ability to
    create highly convincing fake content, including text,
    images, and videos. This could be used to spread
    misinformation or manipulate public opinion
    at scale, potentially undermining democratic
    processes, as well as financial market manipulation.

4. Privacy and Data Protection

    The training of large language models often requires
    vast amounts of data, raising concerns about how
    this data is collected, used, and protected. There
    are also worries about the potential for generative
    AI to produce outputs that reveal personal and
    confidential information.

5. Intellectual Property Rights

    Copyrighted content scraped off the Internet and
    generated by AI raises complex questions about
    intellectual property rights. Regulators are grappling
    with how to protect creators' rights while allowing
    for innovation.

6. Safety and Security

    There are concerns about the potential misuse
    of generative AI for malicious purposes, such as
    creating sophisticated phishing schemes, malware,
    or other cyber threats.

7. Labor Market Disruption

   The increasing capabilities of generative AI could lead to significant changes in the job market, potentially displacing workers in certain industries. Regulators are considering how to manage this transition and ensure social and economic stability.

8. Ethical Considerations

   The development of increasingly sophisticated AI raises broader ethical questions about what sorts of decisions should be entrusted to machines, and the trade-offs made in the name of advancing the common good. Also, the development of powerful generative AI tools is largely concentrated in wealthy nations and tech companies. This raises ethical questions about global equity and the potential for these technologies to exacerbate existing global inequalities.

9. Responsibility and Liability

   As generative AI systems become more autonomous in creating content, there are questions about who is legally responsible for their outputs and any resulting harm or damages.

10. Market Concentration

    The resources required to develop and deploy advanced generative AI systems could lead to market dominance by a few large tech companies, raising antitrust concerns.

11. Education and Skills Gap

     There's a growing need to ensure that the workforce
     is prepared for a future where generative AI plays
     a significant role, which may require changes in
     education and training policies. This is of particular
     concern for regulatory examiners and auditors,
     who may not have a foundational grounding in
     data science in order to evaluate the quality and
     performance of these advanced models.

12. Environmental Impact

     The energy consumption required to train and run
     large AI models is substantial, raising concerns
     about their environmental footprint.

To address these concerns, regulators are considering various
approaches, including:

- Developing new legal and regulatory frameworks
  specifically for AI

- Requiring impact assessments for high-risk AI
  applications

- Mandating transparency in AI decision-making processes

- Establishing guidelines for ethical AI development and use

- Investing in research to better understand the societal
  impacts of generative AI

As the field of generative AI continues to evolve rapidly, regulators
face the challenge of balancing innovation with the need to protect
public interests and mitigate potential risks. Here are some of the early
developments in regulations governing the use of generative AI, by
geographic area/country.

Europe

The first major regulatory initiative was the European Union's AI Act, a comprehensive regulatory framework proposed by the European Union to govern the development, deployment, and use of AI systems first proposed by the European Commission on April 21, 2021. It was adopted by the European Parliament on March 13, 2024, and full application of the act is expected to begin around mid-2026, allowing a transition period for organizations to prepare for compliance [2]

The EU AI Act is extremely broad in scope and applies to many various types of organizations: financial institutions, healthcare providers, educational institutions, manufacturing companies, transportation and logistics firms, retail and e-commerce businesses, and law enforcement agencies; they include the following:[3]

1. AI Providers: Companies that develop and place AI systems on the EU market or put them into service in the EU.

2. AI Users: Organizations that use AI systems within the EU, particularly those using high-risk AI systems.

3. Importers and Distributors: Entities involved in the AI supply chain within the EU.

4. Non-EU Entities: Organizations outside the EU that deploy AI systems whose output is used in the EU.

---

[2] EU AI Act: first regulation on artificial intelligence, published: June 8, 2023, last June 18, 2024 https://www.europarl.europa.eu/topics/en/article/20230601ST093804/eu-ai-act-first-regulation-on-artificial-intelligence

[3] Ibid

5. Public Authorities: Government bodies and
    agencies using AI systems.[4]

Notably, the act is extraterritorial in scope, meaning that organizations outside the EU may need to comply if their AI systems affect individuals in the EU or if the output of their AI systems is used in the EU. There are significant financial penalties for non-compliance, up to €30 million or 6% of global revenues.

For businesses using generative AI, it underscores the importance of responsible AI development and use, with a focus on transparency, fairness, and safety. Generative models used for text, image, or video creation may require clear labeling of AI-generated content.

The act also requires disclosure when AI is used in certain contexts, like chatbots or deep fakes. The act also proscribes strict requirements on training data quality and management could affect generative AI development, provisions against bias and discrimination would apply to generative AI, requiring careful model training and testing and for models rated high-risk, mechanisms to explain outputs may be required.[5]

Asia

On August 15, 2023, China's "Interim Measures for the Management of Generative Artificial Intelligence Services" went into effect, following the publication of the rules by the Cyberspace Administration of China (CAC) on July 13, 2023.[6]

---

[4] Ibid

[5] Ibid

[6] China: Interim Measures on Generative AI enter into force, One Trust Data Guidance, 15 August 2023
    https://www.dataguidance.com/news/china-interim-measures-generative-ai-enter-force

The law specifically applies to the use of generative artificial intelligence (AI) technology to the public within China, meaning that industry organizations, enterprises, educational and scientific research institutions, public cultural institutions, and relevant professional institutions that do not provide content on generative AI tech to the domestic public are not subject to the law.[7]

Another regulatory initiative in Asia is the Monetary Authority of Singapore's Fairness, Ethics, Transparency, and Accountability (FEAT) principles to ensure AI models do not unjustly discriminate against people, promote interpretability of AI-driven decisions, and hold humans accountable for AI-driven decisions and actions.[8]

United States

At the time of this writing, the United States has yet to pass any new laws or issue new regulations governing the development or use of AI.

In terms of guidelines, an important federal initiative is the October 30, 2023, the Biden White House's "Executive Order on the Safe, Secure, and Trustworthy Development and Use of Artificial Intelligence," which offered eight guiding principles and priorities for crafting regulations for AI developers, deployers, and users.

The principles and priorities include provisions for "The responsible development and use of AI require a commitment to supporting American workers. As AI creates new jobs and industries, all workers need a seat

---

[7] Ibid

[8] Principles to Promote Fairness, Ethics, Accountability and Transparency (FEAT) in the Use of Artificial

Intelligence and Data Analytics in Singapore's Financial Sector, The Monetary Authority of Singapore https://www.mas.gov.sg/-/media/mas/news-and-publi-cations/monographs-and-information-papers/feat-principles-updated-7-feb-19.pdf

at the table, including through collective bargaining, to ensure that they benefit from these opportunities," as well as "Artificial Intelligence policies must be consistent with my Administration's dedication to advancing equity and civil rights."[9]

At the state level, nearly 200 new laws were proposed across dozens of states to regulate AI technology, including Utah's new AI transparency law that requires companies to disclose when their AI systems are used to interact with consumers.[10]

Perhaps one of the most consumer-focused regulatory initiatives is Colorado's "Consumer Protections for Artificial Intelligence," which is designed to protect individuals from unfair or inaccurate AI-generated decisions. It states "On and after February 1, 2026, the act requires a developer of a high-risk artificial intelligence system to use reasonable care to protect consumers from any known or reasonably foreseeable risks of algorithmic discrimination in the high-risk system."[11]

Notably, the draft legislation exclusively targets AI-driven decisions affecting consumers, which could range from being denied being hired, promoted, a bank loan or insurance coverage.[12]

---

[9] Executive Order on the Safe, Secure, and Trustworthy Development and Use of Artificial Intelligence, October 30, 2023 https://www.whitehouse.gov/briefing-room/presidential-actions/2023/10/30/executive-order-on-the-safe-secure-and-trustworthy-development-and-use-of-artificial-intelligence/

[10] Utah, Colorado and Other States Lead Groundbreaking AI Legislation in U.S., Davis + Gilbert, May 16, 2024 https://www.dglaw.com/utah-colorado-and-other-states-lead-groundbreaking-ai-legislation-in-u-s/

[11] Consumer Protections for Artificial Intelligence, SB24-205, Colorado General Assembly, Second Regular Session | 74th General Assembly https://leg.colorado.gov/bills/sb24-205

[12] Colorado has a first-in-the-nation law for AI — but what will it do?, Bente Birkeland, CPR News, June 17, 2024 https://www.cpr.org/2024/06/17/colorado-artificial-intelligence-law-implementation-ramifications/

Critics probably view this act as a gold mine for plaintiff's attorneys, who would be able to bring suit on behalf of anyone declined by an algorithm in applying for anything, opening the floodgates of frivolous lawsuits and stifling innovation. Proponents might view the measure as a powerful incentive for organizations to ensure the validity, transparency, fairness, and interpretability of the models they use to make decisions that affect the lives of everyday people.

The Compliance Challenge: Meeting Rising Expectations

As we've noted, the adoption of Gen AI technology means new and expanded organizational roles, functions, and steering committees or governing councils – and their attendant policies, procedures, and supporting documentary evidence – required to comply with existing data privacy laws and regulations, as well as rising social expectations and standards for the proper use of AI.

The key message here: compliance is no small matter when it comes to any form of AI, and organizational leaders need to take it seriously – for everyone's sake.

As a pair of researchers put it in their paper published in the *International Journal for Research in Applied Science and Engineering Technology*, "IT professionals play a crucial role in shaping the ethical landscape of generative AI and ensuring that it aligns with societal values and norms. Security and privacy risks associated with generative AI necessitate robust security measures and privacy protections to safeguard against adversarial attacks and ensure data integrity. Furthermore, the lack of interpretability and transparency in generative AI models poses a challenge to trust and acceptance. IT professionals must work towards improving interpretability and explainability to build trust in generative AI outputs and establish mechanisms for accountability and transparency in their development and use."[13]

The only add we would make there is that it's not just IT professionals who are on the hook; managing these risks is everyone's job in an organization.

Best Practices in Guidelines

For some examples of best practices in guidelines, we suggest the reader check out the following:

- Microsoft's "Empowering Responsible AI Practices" to ensure compliance across its AI products, implementing a system to risk-rated their AI applications based on the definitions in the EU AI Act.[14]

- Google's AI ethics review process for all new AI projects, "AI Governance Reviews and Operations," which included checks for potential biases, environmental impact, and alignment with its AI Principles.[15]

---

[13] Nhavkar, V. K., and K. D. S. Goel. "Impact of Generative AI on IT Professionals." International Journal for Research in Applied Science and Engineering Technology 11, no. 7 (2023): 15-18

[14] Empowering responsible AI Practices, Microsoft, https://www.microsoft.com/en-us/ai/responsible-ai

[15] AI Governance reviews and operations, Google, https://ai.google/responsibility/ai-governance-operations/#:~:text=refine%20our%20process.-,Overview,context%2C%20Google's%20employee%20resource%20groups

- IBM developed and open sourced an AI Fairness 360 toolkit, which it uses internally as well as offer to other organizations for detecting and mitigating bias in AI systems.[16]

- Anthropic's Constitutional AI (CAI) is a crowd-sourced collection of principles written into a constitution to ensure the development of general-purpose language models aligned with the common good.[17]

- Open AI issued its Model Spec guidelines to provide transparency on its approach to shaping model behavior and invite public input about how its methods for ensuring model outputs meet ethical and responsible standards can be improved.[18]

Model Governance Comes to the Fore

Model governance is a set of disciplines to ensure the accuracy of model inputs and outputs, how models are designed and implemented, and that the potential financial and operational risks are identified and managed.

Back in the day when most models used by financial institutions were relatively simple, stand-alone decision-support systems, the model risk management function was relegated to the backwaters of the middle-office, inhabited by mid-level bureaucrats and quant nerds.

---

[16] AI Fairness 360, IBM Developer Staff, November 14, 2018, https://www.ibm.com/opensource/open/projects/ai-fairness-360/

[17] Collective Constitutional AI: Aligning a Language Model with Public Input, Anthropic, October 17, 2023 https://www.anthropic.com/news/collective-constitutional-ai-aligning-a-language-model-with-public-input

[18] Model Spec, Open AI, May 6, 2024 https://cdn.openai.com/spec/model-spec-2024-05-08.html

Today, model governance is now emerging in finance and other industries as a major player, taking on much greater visibility as well as prominence in the age of Gen AI.

The Fed's Guidelines

Perhaps the best-known set of standards is the Federal Reserve Board's SR 11-7: Guidance on Model Risk Management for banks and bank-holding companies that outlines standard practices for three core functions:[19]

1. **Model development, implementation, and use** to ensure the sound design, theory, and logic underlying models; robust model methodologies for their design and testing, rigorous assessment of data quality and relevance, and appropriate documentation.

2. **Model validation** to verify that models are performing as expected, in line with their design objectives and business uses, ensuring that models are sound, identifying potential limitations and assumptions and assessing their possible impact.

3. **Governance, policies, and controls** to ensure that model risk management function at the banks have adequate policies that define relevant risk management activities, have procedures to implement those policies, and allocate resources and mechanisms to test compliance with those policies and procedures through their organizations.

---

[19] SR 11-7: Guidance on Model Risk Management, Federal Reserve Board, April 4, 2011 https://www.federalreserve.gov/supervisionreg/srletters/sr1107.htm

Moreover, the guidance mandates that "Model risk governance is provided at the highest level by the board of directors and senior management when they establish an organization-wide approach to model risk management."[20]

Other standards and practices for model governance include the AI Risk Management Framework from the National Institute of Standards and Technology (NIST)[21] and Guidance for Safe Foundation Model Deployment by the Partnership on AI, a coalition of major tech companies and research institutions focused on generative AI governance.[22]

Types of Model Risks

As outlined in earlier chapters of this book, there are a number of risks that emerge as organizations integrate machine learning and AI analytics solutions into business decision-making processes. They include

1. Bias and Fairness: Models may perpetuate or amplify existing biases in training data.

2. Lack of Transparency: Complex models (especially deep learning) can be "black boxes," making it difficult to explain decisions.

3. Data Privacy: Many models require large amounts of potentially sensitive data.

4. Model Drift: As real-world conditions change, model performance can degrade over time.

---

[20] Ibid

[21] AI Risk Management Framework from The National Institute of Standards and Technology (NIST) https://www.nist.gov/itl/ai-risk-management-framework

[22] Guidance for Safe Foundation Model Deployment, The Partnership on AI, https://partnershiponai.org/modeldeployment/

5. Overreliance: There's a risk of over-trusting model outputs without appropriate human oversight.

6. Security Vulnerabilities: AI models can be targets for adversarial attacks or data poisoning.

7. Reputational and Regulatory Risk: Failure to adhere to emerging AI regulations can lead to legal or regulatory issues. Ensuring fair and unbiased decision-making is crucial for maintaining public trust and avoiding reputational damage, which often requires transparency and interpretability, as stakeholders increasingly demand understanding of how AI-driven decisions are made.

The Many Faces of Model Risk Management

Model risk manifests itself in many different ways based on complexity and type. Below are some examples of functions involved in managing model risk.

1. Financial Risk Management

    – Model Risk: Financial institutions need to expand their model risk management frameworks to specifically address AI and machine learning models. This includes more rigorous validation processes for AI models used in credit scoring, trading, and fraud detection.

    – Regulatory Capital: Some banking regulators are considering how AI risks should be factored into capital requirements, potentially leading to higher capital buffers for institutions heavily reliant on AI systems.

- Financial Stress Testing: AI-specific scenarios were being incorporated into stress testing exercises to ensure banks that use AI can withstand severe systemic economic shocks.

2. Operational Risk Management

- AI Incident Response: Organizations have developed specific protocols for AI-related incidents, such as model failures or unexpected outputs from generative AI systems.

- Third-Party Risk: With increased use of AI vendors, third-party risk management processes have been enhanced to include AI-specific due diligence and ongoing monitoring.

- Cybersecurity: AI-powered cybersecurity tools have become more prevalent, but also introduced new risks that needed to be managed, such as potential vulnerabilities in AI models themselves.

3. Model Risk Governance

- Model Inventory: Organizations have expanded their model inventories to specifically identify and categorize AI models, including details on training data, model architecture, and intended use.

- Model Documentation: More comprehensive documentation requirements have been implemented for AI models, including details on training processes, testing procedures, and known limitations.

- Model Monitoring: Continuous monitoring practices have been enhanced to detect issues like model drift, bias, or unexpected behaviors in AI systems.

4. Model Policy Requirements

- AI Ethics Policies: Many organizations have implemented specific AI ethics policies, outlining principles for responsible AI development and use.

- Data Governance: Policies around data use and privacy have been updated to address the unique challenges posed by AI, particularly regarding training data for generative models.

- Explainable AI: Policies requiring a certain level of interpretability for AI-driven decisions, especially in areas like lending or insurance underwriting, have become more common.

5. Procedures and Review Committees

- AI Impact Assessments: Similar to privacy impact assessments, many organizations have implemented AI impact assessment procedures for new AI projects.

- Model Review Committees: Cross-functional committees to review and approve high-risk AI models have been established in many firms.

- Audit Procedures: Internal audit functions have developed new procedures specifically for auditing AI systems and their governance.

6. Regulatory Reporting

    –   Some financial regulators have started requiring specific reporting on AI use and associated risks. For example, the European Banking Authority was working on guidelines for AI use in the financial sector, which included reporting requirements.

7. Training and Awareness

    –   Organizations have increased training efforts to ensure that risk management and compliance staff are equipped to handle AI-specific challenges.

Summary

The adoption of Gen AI technology means new and expanded organizational roles, functions, and steering committees – and their attendant policies, procedures, and supporting documentary evidence – required to comply with the new laws, regulations, guidelines, and industry standards.

CHAPTER 8

Views from the Ivory Tower

Research is seeing what everybody else has seen and thinking what nobody else has thought.

—Dr. Albert Szent-Györgyi, Nobel Prize winner and cofounder of the National Foundation for Cancer Research

Gen AI and the rise of intelligent machines have become hot topics in academia, the subject of countless research studies by social scientists, organizational behaviorists, economists, and a full range of academics in the applied sciences.

This chapter shifts through research findings from various academic disciplines to highlight some of the more notable ones. We first will cover the general trends and then cite the findings of specific research papers.

The Coming Boom That Didn't Happen (Yet)

Perhaps as a preamble or disclaimer before discussing the results of some of these academic research studies, we should note that not all findings – even from prominent institutions of higher learning – should be taken at face value.

© Arthur J. O'Connor 2024
A. J. O'Connor, *Organizing for Generative AI and the Productivity Revolution*,
https://doi.org/10.1007/979-8-8688-0959-0_8

That is, we remind the reader that consultants, the media, corporations, and tech vendors aren't the only parties guilty of hyping Gen AI. As a prime example of this, we cite the highly publicized research paper entitled "The Coming Productivity Boom" from MIT and Stanford professors, who came up with the term "The Productivity Paradox." [1]

The term was conceived to explain why – despite the widespread use of chatbots in recent years and their alleged time-saving benefits – increases in labor productivity had yet to appear in the numbers, notably the figures reported by the US Bureau of Labor Statistics.

To explain the absence of statistical evidence, the researchers at MIT and Stanford offered the following theory: in the early stages of a major new technology revolution, productivity initially **declines** as the improvements in efficiency and effectiveness don't yet manifest in the numbers, given the need for organizations to make significant investments to move up the learning curve and reengineer their processes (hence, the paradox).[2]

As empirical evidence to support their theory, the researchers pointed out that while labor productivity growth in the United States averaged only 1.3% since 2006 – less than half the rate of the previous decade – productivity growth increased by 5.4% in the first quarter of 2021, which they saw as a precursor to the productivity boom to come.[3]

However, since that research was published, the annual percent increase in non-farm labor productivity growth from the prior quarter (the line in the chart below) **declined** over the following quarters in 2021, and actually turned **negative** before turning positive again, starting in the third quester of 2022, but well below the 5.4% rate – as shown in Figure 8-1.[4]

---

[1] "The coming productivity boom," Erik Brynjolfsson and Georgios Petropoulos, MIT Technology Review, June 10, 2021, https://www.technologyreview.com/2021/06/10/1026008/the-coming-productivity-boom/

[2] Ibid

[3] Ibid

[4] US Bureau of Labor Statistics, Productivity and Costs, First Quarter Revised, June 6, 2024, https://www.bls.gov/news.release/pdf/prod2.pdf

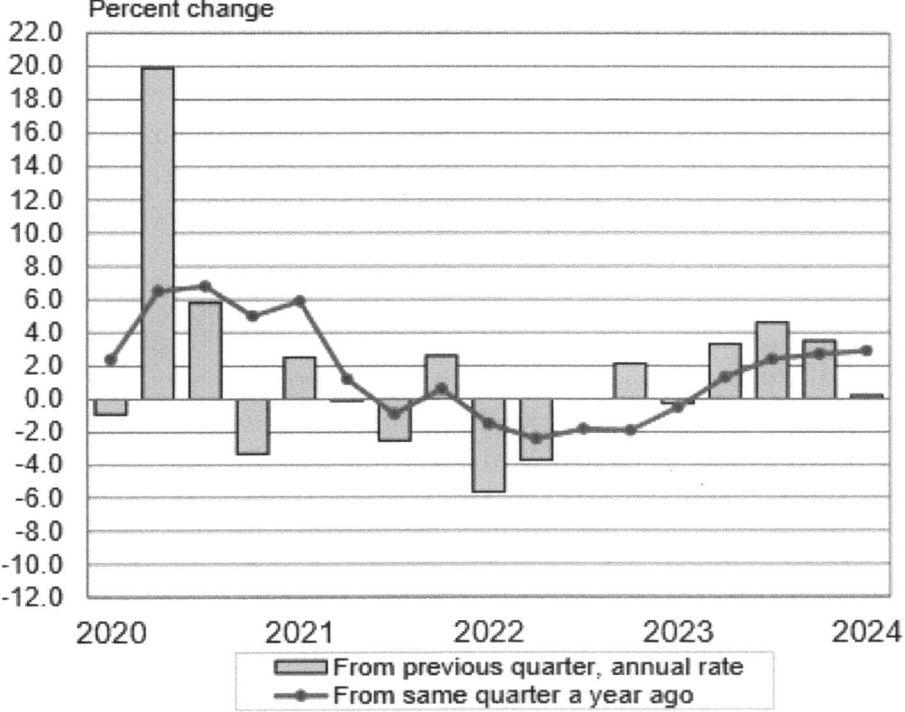

Figure 8-1. *Labor productivity, non-farm business, 2020 Q1–2024 Q1*

In other words, the coming productivity boom predicted by researchers at MIT and Stanford – if or when it does materialize – may take far more time to show up in the numbers from the US Bureau of Labor Statistics.

The Research Landscape Overview

Taking a step back and examining the body of academic literature as a whole, the common themes about the diffusion of Gen AI technologies in the workplace center around, on one hand, fears about massive labor market displacement, and on the other, the promise of increased worker productivity and liberation from repetitive, routine tasks.

Drilling down in more detail, the concerns include increasing income inequality from a wage premium for workers who can effectively utilize and manage AI tools, the commoditization of knowledge or white-collar work – occupations once regarded as the keys to upward mobility, now reduced to electronic gig work – and the leakage of company confidential information and threats to intellectual property rights (lack of attribution and compensation for use of proprietary material).

These concerns are counterbalanced with the promise of massive gains in productivity and innovations that free employees to focus on more creative, collaborative, and even altruistic pursuits.

Notably, very few research studies directly address the many practical issues that arise in implementing these technologies in mission-critical business processes.

Hype and Despair

In their 2024 paper published in Social Science Research Network, academics John Zysman and Mark Nitzberg stated their objective of their study on the potential impact of Gen AI systems – in light of the sci-fi-like buzz – both optimism about improving the quality of work life as well as pessimism over destroying jobs – was to "…move beyond hype and despair."[5]

They predict that the use of AI will vary greatly by industry sector, "Firms in sectors such as professional services, materials, and pharmaceuticals seem to have particular exposure to the use of Generative AI tools," but that the rate and scope of organizational adaptations will "…depend greatly on who controls the decisions about deployment."[6]

---

[5] Generative AI and the Future of Work: Augmentation or Automation? John Zysman, Mark Nitzberg, Social Science Research Network, 2024
[6] Ibid

The authors argue that the current limitations of AI tools require humans to remain in the loop – not just to prevent mistakes but also to maximize its potential to create value. "Maintaining the centrality of humans is likely to prove crucial—in training systems, curating data, and assessing outputs." They conclude that, "Ultimately, avoiding a dystopian scenario might hinge on fostering new norms in which human capabilities remain essential."[7]

Outperforming Wall Street Research Analysts

A working paper from three researchers at the University of Chicago Booth business school found that a popular LLM did a better job than human investment analysts at predicting whether the earnings of publicly traded companies would increase or decrease from the prior year, a key influence on their respective stock prices.

Based on its review of financial statements of 15,401 companies from 1968 to 2021 – without the benefit of any industry-specific information or company-provided narratives at Wall Street conferences or quarterly earnings calls – the LLM correctly predicted whether a company's earnings would grow or shrink in the subsequent year by 60.35% of the time. By comparison, human-generated predictions on the same types of financial information for 3,152 companies from 1983 to 2021 were accurate by 52.71%, or only a little better than half of the time.[8]

---

[7] Ibid

[8] Kim, Alex G. and Muhn, Maximilian and Nikolaev, Valeri V., Financial Statement Analysis with Large Language Models (May 20, 2024). Chicago Booth Research Paper, Fama-Miller Working Paper, Available at SSRN: https://ssrn.com/abstract=4835311 or

Interestingly, however, the LLM's predictive accuracy fell during periods of exogenous shocks to the economy, such as the 1974 oil embargo, the 2008 financial crisis, and the Covid-19 pandemic. The researchers concluded that since the LLM's forecasts are based exclusively on financial statements, human analysts are better at predicting when exogenous factors become more powerful influences.[9]

"Astonishing" Productivity Increases

As one might expect, most research studies have found positive impacts on worker productivity through the use of Gen AI, with less-experienced workers benefiting the most gains.

In software development, coders using GitHub's Copilot completed tasks 56% faster than the control group, and developers with less programming experience exhibited the greatest improvement.[10]

Similarly, ChatGPT has been shown to increase the productivity of writers, particularly those with lower abilities.[11] In customer service, agents using an AI-assistant increased their productivity by 14%, with novices and low-skilled workers benefiting disproportionately.[12]

In an experiment conducted by the Boston Consulting Group – working with scholars from Harvard Business School, MIT Sloan School of Management, the Wharton School at the University of Pennsylvania, and the University of Warwick – researchers described the increase in

---

[9] Ibid

[10] Peng, S., Kalliamvakou, E., Cihon, P., & Demirer, M. (2023). The impact of AI on developer productivity: Evidence from github copilot. arXiv preprint arXiv:2302.06590

[11] Brynjolfsson, E., Li, D., & Raymond, L. R. (2023). Generative AI at work (No. w31161). National Bureau of Economic Research

[12] Noy, S., & Zhang, W. (2023). Experimental evidence on the productivity effects of generative artificial intelligence. Available at SSRN 4375283

productivity of the professional services firms' 750 BCG consultants worldwide using Open AI's GPT-4 for certain types of tasks as nothing short of "astonishing." [13]

"When using generative AI (in our experiment, OpenAI's GPT-4) for creative product innovation, a task involving ideation and content creation, around 90% of our participants improved their performance. What's more, they converged on a level of performance that was 40% higher than that of those working on the same task without GPT-4."[14]

The study noted that the current generation to Gen AI tools have distinct strengths and weaknesses. In short, it's great for brainstorming; not so good for problem-solving. "Creative ideation sits firmly within Gen AI's current frontier of competence. When our participants used the technology for business problem solving, a capability outside this frontier, they performed 23% worse than those doing the task without GPT-4."[15]

Or as some other researchers put it, "AI is good at generating new combinations of existing ideas, rather than making conceptual leaps." [16]

In examining the productivity effects of a generative AI technology for routine business writing, researchers tasked 453 college-educated professionals to write short stories. Half were exposed to ChatGPT; the other half were not.[17] Not surprisingly, the productivity of the ChatGPT users was 40% greater than the non-AI users, while output quality improved 18%.[18]

---

[13] Candelon, Francois, Lisa Krayer, Saran Rajendran, and David Zuluaga Martinez. "How People Can Create–and Destroy–Value with Generative AI." BCG Global 21 (2023)

[14] Ibid

[15] Ibid

[16] Frey, Carl Benedikt, and Michael Osborne. "Generative AI and the future of work: a reappraisal." Brown Journal of World Affairs 30, no. 1 (2024), p. 3

[17] Shakked Noy, Whitney Zhang, Experimental evidence on the productivity effects of generative artificial intelligence. Science 381,187-192(2023). DOI:10.1126/science.adh2586

[18] Ibid

The study also found that participants assigned to use ChatGPT were more productive, efficient, and enjoyed the tasks more. Participants with weaker skills benefited the most from ChatGPT, which lead the researchers to postulate the technology's potential to reduce productivity inequality.

Interestingly, while the employees using ChatGPT reported that they were twice as likely to use it at their job immediately after the experiment, they were only 1.6 times as likely to use it when surveyed two months following the trial – perhaps as indication of users learning the risks and limitations of the current generation of chatbots.

Employee Well-Being and Job Enrichment

In an industry-focused study, researchers reported the application of current generation of Gen AI tools as having an immense impact on the hospitality and tourism industry, and in particular, supply chain management, customer relationship management, compliance with safety and security regulation, and employee satisfaction through the automation of repetitive and routine tasks.[19]

While noting that this industry traditionally has been slow to adopt new technology, the researchers predict "...Chat GPT will not completely replace personnel in the hospitality and tourism industry but rather augment them and enhance employee productivity. It will also give them the freedom to shift from monotonous work to more meaningful customer-related job responsibilities. This would help enhance the well-being and job enrichment of employees in the hospitality and tourism sector in the long run."[20]

---

[19] Dwivedi, Yogesh K., Neeraj Pandey, Wendy Currie, and Adrian Micu. "Leveraging ChatGPT and other generative artificial intelligence (AI)-based applications in the hospitality and tourism industry: practices, challenges and research agenda." International Journal of Contemporary Hospitality Management 36, no. 1 (2024): 1-12

[20] Ibid

In contrast, a group of academics from Penn State, University of Florida, and the State University of New York interviewed 18 Gen AI users in creative fields – art, public relations, design, marketing, and research and technology – and found that while Gen AI have great potential to leverage and complement human expertise, they noted that many users express uncertainties regarding the ownership of intellectual property of content co-created with Gen AI, the risks of confidential information being exposed in prompts querying open source LLMs, and compliance with regulations and laws in some jurisdictions that prohibit their use.[21]

The Ironies of Automation

But perhaps most intriguing were the findings by a group of researchers in the United Kingdom who found the opposite: some workers are actually becoming less productive, a phenomenon they call "the ironies of automation." Or as the authors put it, "...a tendency for automation to make easy tasks easier and hard tasks harder."[22]

The researchers reviewed over 30 years of Human Factors research (a multidisciplinary field that studies how people interact with systems, equipment, and processes to improve safety, performance, and user satisfaction) and outlined the different ways by which new labor-saving technologies have historically impeded improvements in labor productivity. Factors include overwhelming users' abilities to operate, oversee, and evaluate the performance of new, highly sophisticated

---

[21] Sun, Yuan, Eunchae Jang, Fenglong Ma, and Ting Wang. "Generative AI in the Wild: Prospects, Challenges, and Strategies." In Proceedings of the CHI Conference on Human Factors in Computing Systems, pp. 1-16. 2024

[22] Simkute, Auste, Lev Tankelevitch, Viktor Kewenig, Ava Elizabeth Scott, Abigail Sellen, and Sean Rintel. "Ironies of Generative AI: Understanding and mitigating productivity loss in human-AI interactions." arXiv preprint arXiv:2402.11364 (2024)

systems, as well as poor human interface design that degrades usability and disrupts and interrupt user workflows, which further overloads users' cognitive capacity and undermines potential for productivity gains.

The authors suggest how Human Factors research can benefit Gen AI system design to mitigate productivity loss by using approaches such as continuous feedback, system personalization, ecological interface design, task stabilization, and clear task allocation.

IBM's Design Principles

To that point – improving the usability of Gen AI tools – a group of researchers at IBM set forth six design principles for generative AI applications, based on reviews of prior research, input from designers, and testing of these design principles in two real-world generative AI applications.

The guidelines for human-AI interaction are as follows:[23]

1. Design Responsibly: Ensure the AI system solves real user issues and minimizes user harms.

2. Design for Generative Variability: Help the user manage the ability of generative models to produce multiple outputs that are distinct and varied.

3. Design for Mental Models: Communicate how to work effectively with the AI system, considering the user's background and goals.

---

[23] Weisz, Justin D., Jessica He, Michael Muller, Gabriela Hoefer, Rachel Miles, and Werner Geyer. "Design Principles for Generative AI Applications." In Proceedings of the CHI Conference on Human Factors in Computing Systems, pp. 1-22. 2024

4. Design for Co-creation: Enable the user to influence the generative process and work collaboratively with the AI system.

5. Design for Appropriate Trust and Reliance: Help the user determine when they should or should not rely on the AI system's outputs by teaching them to be skeptical of quality issues, inaccuracies, biases, underrepresentation, and other issues.

6. Design for Imperfection: Help the user understand and work with outputs that may not align with their expectations

Techno-Stress

There are many other research studies that are not so constructive or upbeat in their results and findings.

In their study of the impact of AI on employees working in "Industry 4.0-led organizations," researchers interviewed 32 professionals with average work experience of 7.6 years and working across nine industries to develop a practical understanding of the positive and negative employee experiences due to artificial intelligence adoption.

Their findings note key adverse impacts of the adoption of AI, particularly the "...drastic changes resulting from digital transformations and job risk and insecurity brewing in the employee psyche." The researchers called the phenomenon "techno-stress."[24]

---

[24] Malik, Nishtha, Shalini Nath Tripathi, Arpan Kumar Kar, and Shivam Gupta. "Impact of artificial intelligence on employees working in industry 4.0 led organizations." International Journal of Manpower 43, no. 2 (2021): 334-354

On a far more positive note, the researchers pointed out potential benefits of flexibility and autonomy, creativity and innovation, and overall job enrichment.[25]

Based on their findings, the researchers recommended that employers "...deploy strategic manpower development measures involving up-gradation of skills and knowledge management."[26]

In a similar study, researchers at Google and Cal State decided to look at how knowledge workers feel about job transformation. In their 2024 study entitled, "How Knowledge Workers Think Generative AI Will (Not) Transform Their Industries," they conducted focus groups to gain a better understanding how knowledge workers expect generative AI may affect their industries in the future.

Based on these workshops that included 54 participants from seven different industries across three US cities, they found a surprising lack of understanding and awareness of even the current generation of capabilities, noting that "...participants largely envision generative AI as a tool to perform menial work, under human review. Participants do not generally anticipate the disruptive changes to knowledge industries currently projected in common media and academic narratives."[27]

Despite their generally dismissive view of the technology, the majority of participants expressed deep fears about Gen AI's potential impact. "Participants do however envision generative AI may amplify four social forces currently shaping their industries: deskilling, dehumanization, disconnection, and disinformation."

Woof!

---

[25] Ibid

[26] Ibid

[27] Woodruff, Allison, Renee Shelby, Patrick Gage Kelley, Steven Rousso-Schindler, Jamila Smith-Loud, and Lauren Wilcox. "How knowledge workers think generative ai will (not) transform their industries." In Proceedings of the CHI Conference on Human Factors in Computing Systems, pp. 1-26. 2024

Perhaps those findings at least help explain the emphasis many organizations are placing on AI literacy, prompt engineering, and the ability to safely and effectively interact with AI systems.

The study concluded employee perceptions and attitudes toward AI influence their responses to its use. "More positive attitudes will likely result in efforts to upskill and functionally use the technology, whereas more negative attitudes will likely result in resistance and poor uptake."[28]

In a similar vein, a 2021 research study published in the Journal of Theoretical and Applied Electronic Commerce Research, researchers created an online survey to explore how workers with different mindsets will likely respond to AI-driven organizational changes.[29]

Based on a questionnaire in the survey, the researchers categorized the respondents into four groups: skeptics, doubtful skeptics, optimists, and doubtful optimists.

The findings showed doubtful optimists to be the most able to affect organizational adoption and positively influence skeptics and doubtful skeptics. Accordingly, the researchers recommended that senior management promoting AI-driven organizational changes target their communication efforts on this group.[30]

---

[28] A multilevel review of artificial intelligence in organizations: Implications for organizational behavior research and practice, Sarah Bankins, A. C. Ocampo, Mauricio Marrone, S. Restubog, S. E. Woo, Journal of Organizational Behavior, 2023

[29] Organizational Structure and Artificial Intelligence. Modeling the Intraorganizational Response to the AI Contingency, I. Rudko, Aysan Bashirpour Bonab, Francesco Bellini, Journal of Theoretical and Applied Electronic Commerce Research, 2021

[30] Ibid

The "Orgmind"

In pondering what the future human-machine collaborative organization will look like, a researcher in Singapore notes that survival in the brave new world "...requires all intelligent human organizations to be designed around intelligence."[31]

Observing that "...an intelligent structure is vital to all businesses as the world moves deeper into the knowledge economy," the author proposes the concept of the "orgmind," defined as "the collection of all the interacting human thinking systems" constantly and fully aware of both internal and external environments.[32]

The researcher concludes, "Inevitably, in the new economy, intelligent human organizations must be equipped with a well-integrated intelligent information network which functions similarly to the nervous system in biological beings."[33]

Summary

In summary, social scientists and organizational behaviorists have found that generative AI is leading to significant transformations:

> Productivity: studies have shown significant
> productivity gains in organizations that effectively
> implement generative AI tools. However, these
> gains are not uniform across all sectors, job types,
> and tasks.

---

[31] Yick, Liang Thow. "The Crucial Roles of the Artificial Information Systems Web in Intelligent Human Organizations." 1 Jan. 2003 : 115 – 124
[32] Ibid
[33] Ibid

Job Satisfaction: Research has found that AI can significantly influence worker well-being, with the potential to enhance job satisfaction.

Organizational Structure: Some studies suggest that AI is facilitating flatter organizational structures by reducing the need for middle management with de-centralized and more collaborative decision-making.

Organizational Behavior: Studies have shown that successful AI adoption often requires significant changes in organizational culture, promoting openness to innovation and continuous learning, with many employers updating and expanding their educational and training programs to keep pace with employee AI competencies.

Governance: Studies in information systems and computer science have highlighted the need for new governance structures to manage AI use in organizations, including issues of data privacy, algorithmic bias, and ethical decision-making.

Process Redesign: Studies in operations management have focused on how business processes are being redesigned to incorporate AI tools, often leading to significant changes in workflow and job descriptions.

Leadership: Studies in leadership and management note that creativity, empathy, critical thinking, and adaptability have become as important – or perhaps even more important – than technical skills in the era of intelligent machines.

However, we must note, not all organizational effects are going to be positive. As you've seen in prior chapters, the implementation of Gen AI is no cake walk. Despite its many potential benefits, the integration of generative AI into existing organizational structures poses significant challenges.[34]

---

[34] Dwivedi, Yogesh K., Laurie Hughes, Elvira Ismagilova, Gert Aarts, Crispin Coombs, Tom Crick, Yanqing Duan et al. "Artificial Intelligence (AI): Multidisciplinary perspectives on emerging challenges, opportunities, and agenda for research, practice and policy." International journal of information management 57 (2021): 101994

CHAPTER 9

Preparing for the Next Big Thing

You don't need an AI strategy, you need a business strategy for AI.[1]

—Colette Stallbaumer, general manager, Microsoft

If you've made it this far in the book, we hope you feel that you've achieved a better understanding of both the organizational requirements and challenges of implementing generative AI, as well as some of the environmental influences driving them.

In this final chapter, we review what we've covered and talk a bit about the inherent danger in separating knowledge from understanding – given our ability now to get answers to questions without our needing to understand the context, meaning, implications, or in some cases, the relevance or accuracy of response generated – but also discuss its tremendous potential of generative AI.

---

[1] "You don't need an AI strategy, you need a business strategy for AI," M. Moore, Tech Radar Pro, June 16, 2024. https://www.techradar.com/pro/you-dont-need-an-ai-strategy-you-need-a-business-strategy-for-ai-microsoft-tells-us-why-utilizing-ai-at-work-could-not-only-make-you-more-productive-but-happier-too

© Arthur J. O'Connor 2024
A. J. O'Connor, *Organizing for Generative AI and the Productivity Revolution*, https://doi.org/10.1007/979-8-8688-0959-0_9

We end the book with a "pre-flight checklist" for managers to undertake this bold adventure for the first time.

To start this final chapter, perhaps it's best to take a step back and consider the profound implications of this productivity revolution, examining both the upsides and downsides.

We start with the downsides.

Upstairs, Downstairs

In a recent survey by freelancing platform Upwork, based on a poll of 2,500 workers in the United States, United Kingdom, Australia, and Canada to examine how AI has impacted the workplace – half of whom are company executives; the other half are full-time employees or freelancers – the study found that while 96% of executives expect AI to boost worker productivity, almost half (47%) of employees using AI say they have no idea how to achieve the productivity gains their employers expect.[2]

If that wasn't bad enough, 77% of the rank and file surveyed reported that the tools have actually decreased their productivity and added to their workload.[3]

Building upon the Microsoft GM's quote that introduces this final chapter, we offer this observation as a possible explanation for the upstairs/downstairs disconnect: perhaps at least some of the confusion and anxieties about applying Gen AI stem from the fact that many organizations appear to be attempting to develop an AI strategy without fully understanding what type of organizational model they need, instead of a business strategy for AI, which would require a re-engineering of their operating model.

---

[2] "From Burnout to Balance: AI-Enhanced Work Models," Upwork Research Institute, Jul 23, 2024 `https://www.upwork.com/research/ai-enhanced-work-models`
[3] Ibid

That is, some business leaders upstairs seem more interested in "getting with the times" and simply force-fitting AI models into their current business processes, without first re-thinking and designing their operations and organizations (for the staff working downstairs) around AI-enabled business strategies.

In the corporate world, the sunny promises oozing from company press releases about management's bold embrace of these new technologies represent much of the same old bovine excrement they've served up so many times before: becoming a data-driven organization, embracing a new paradigm of empowerment and employee engagement, creating a culture of innovation and continuous learning, and automating routine or repetitive tasks to unleash the creativity and realize the full potential of staff – ad nauseam.[4]

And this herd mentality is not helpful. In some cases, it's giving the technology a bad rep.

"AI Washing"

There's even a new buzzword for organizations' exaggerating their embrace of AI: "AI Washing."

A variant of "greenwashing" – the practice of company's making false or misleading claims about their environmentally friendly policies and actions (which in turn is a variant of "whitewashing," defined as deliberately concealing unpleasant or ugly aspects about someone or something) – "AI washing" was coined by the US Securities and Exchange Commission (SEC) to describe practices where firms embellish or exaggerate their use of AI in their disclosures to attract investors by creating an illusion of innovation or competitive advantage.

---

[4] The author apologizes for readers who find this passage a bit too snarky. As one reader said: "This reads like it was written by mob character played by Joe Pesci."

In March 2024, the SEC charged two investment advisers for making false and misleading statements about their purported use of AI. In its press release, the SEC stated: "We've seen time and again that when new technologies come along, they can create buzz from investors as well as false claims by those purporting to use those new technologies. Investment advisers should not mislead the public by saying they are using an AI model when they are not. Such AI washing hurts investors."[5]

Disrupter vs. Distractor

Gen AI may prove to be a seminal movement in industrial automation history and an industry disrupter, but, according to a recent *WSJ* story, it's also proving to be a distractor.

The article reports that – due to all the hype – many CIOs and CTOs are getting bombarded by requests to find ways to integrate Gen AI, which is crowding out other technologies, some of which are cheaper and far more appropriate – and as simple as spreadsheets.[6]

For functions such as demand forecasting, anomaly detection, predictive maintenance, and churn prediction, for example, generative AI may be overkill – and far more expensive, and less accurate and effective – than classic machine or deep learning techniques. It's like choosing a sledgehammer to swat flies.

Exhibit A of a misapplication comes from McDonald's – perhaps an example of an insufficient understanding of the accuracy of current voice recognition tools, as well as the dubious economics of supplanting

---

[5] SEC Charges Two Investment Advisers with Making False and Misleading Statements About Their Use of Artificial Intelligence, U.S. Securities and Exchange Commission, March 18, 2024 https://www.sec.gov/newsroom/press-releases/2024-36

[6] "A Clamor for Generative AI (Even If Something Else Works Better)," Isabelle Bousquette, *WSJ* https://www.wsj.com/articles/a-clamor-for-generative-ai-even-if-something-else-works-better-d9bd0257?mod=djemCIO

low-wage workers with expensive technology. The fast food chain rolled out its AI drive through system to over 100 locations, only to withdraw the system due to mistakes in about 20% of the food orders, which then had to be corrected manually.[7]

At least some of this confusion is understandable, as most business folks aren't all that familiar with relative strengths and applicability of various data analytics, machine learning, neural networks, and other types of statistical and AI tools – much less how they differ from generative AI.

The Right Tool for the Right Job

Truth is, many types of (non-generative AI) models are generally better suited to different types of tasks. Examples include

- Convolutional Neural Networks for computer vision, which process pixel data, identifying patterns and features within images

- K-Means Clustering, which partitions data into groups based on similarity used for customer segmentation

- Reinforcement Learning, which trains agents by giving rewards or penalties to achieve an objective, used in robotics

- Support Vector Machines, which find the optimal path separating data points into different classes

---

[7] "McDonald's Pulls the Plug on Its AI-Powered Order-Taking Technology," Lea Mira, Restaurant Technology News, June 14, 2024 https://restaurant technologynews.com/2024/06/mcdonalds-pulls-the-plug-on-its-ai-powered-order-taking-technology/

- Decision Trees and Random Forests that create tree-like models of decisions and their possible consequences, used for classification and regression

Some of the more popular libraries used for machine learning are Pandas for data manipulation and analysis, Matplotlib and Shiny for data visualization and dashboards, NumPy and SciPy for scientific computing, and Scikit-learn, which features various algorithms and tools for various tasks, including classification, regression, clustering, and dimensionality reduction.

For building and training neural networks, the most popular frameworks seem to be PyTorch, Keras, and TensorFlow.

What Makes Gen AI Different

So how does one know when Gen AI is the right tool for the job? Here's a key difference.

The examples and software libraries above are primarily used for decision support; they're about helping humans gain insights from manipulating data.

A key difference is that Gen AI models **create** content by inference based on their training data and the weights and parameters from which it has learned (which is how they become "intelligent").

Thus, instead of merely helping humans make more informed decisions (which it also can be used for), generative AI models **generate** things...

- Detailed diagnoses of patient conditions, based on millions of medical files and personal case histories

- Insightful responses to customer inquiries based on client profiles, product or service details, and histories of similar customer complaints or questions or transactions

- Images, videos, and/or illustrations of anything a user can imagine and articulate

…and generally, any task that requires shifting through gazillions of permutations and possibilities, calculating the probabilities relative to countless constraints and parameters, to arrive at an optimal solution within seconds or minutes that would take researchers days, weeks, months, and even years to do.

The Right Metrics

With the focus on labor-saving productivity gains and cost reduction, Ricardo Baeza-Yates, Director of Research at the Institute for Experiential AI of Northeastern University, wonders if we as a society are focusing enough of what we **should** be creating Gen AI to do rather than what the technology **can** do.

"Responsible AI isn't a buzzword, he writes, "It's a commitment to making the world a better place."[8]

"Do we have the right evaluation techniques for defining what we want AI to do?" He suggests that instead of narrowly focusing on a single average like accuracy or perplexity in LLM benchmarks, perhaps we should pay more attention in advancing the common good and avoiding harm as performance criteria.

---

[8] Baeza-Yates R. LECTURE HELD AT THE ACADEMIA EUROPAEA BUILDING BRIDGES CONFERENCE 2022: An Introduction to Responsible AI. European Review. 2023;31(4):406-421. doi:10.1017/S1062798723000145

From the Same Nice Folks Who Gave Us Surveillance Capitalism

For what it's worth, we share many of these same concerns.

After all, many of the Masters of the Universe from Silicon Valley (presumably our best and brightest tech minds) who created these massive models come from the same big tech firms that gave us Surveillance Capitalism, the wildly successful business model that creates vast wealth and power by spying on its users to discern behavioral patterns and profiles in order to pander to their tendencies, biases, and buying habits.

The Risk of Mediocrity

Baeza-Yates points out another danger of Gen AI: the spread of mediocrity. While computers aren't inherently lazy, many humans are. He refers to an essay by Ray Nadler, a visiting scholar at the George Washington University's Institute of International Science and Technology Policy, who describes Gen AI as "...effective when we need regurgitation of the commonplace... and writing passable, if bland, essays on many basic topics."[9]

As Gen AI makes it incredibly easy to produce memos, emails, articles, reports, analyses that are derived, remixed, and repackaged from what was done before, the essay asks, will we humans slack off, defaulting to the quick, sufficient, and mediocre with minimal effort instead of striving for the creative, inspired, and original?

As Nadler puts it: "....everything that predictive language and image models will produce will be a sequel to what came before: not an original idea, but a mash-up of our old tropes, repackaged for our consumption.

---

[9] "AI and the Rise of Mediocrity," Ray Nayler, Time, November 27, 2023 `https://time.com/6337835/ai-mediocrity-essay/`

This was already a dominant tendency in our commercial industries—to simply take what has been done before, tweak it a little, rebrand it, and call it new."[10]

And the dangers of separating knowledge from understanding are worth considering.

The Decline of Deep Understanding and Critical Thinking?

Until recently in human history, knowledge – the accumulation of facts, information, and skills acquired through experience or education – was intrinsically connected to understanding, the ability to comprehend the meaning, context, and implications of that knowledge.

Generative AI disrupts this classic relationship by enabling the rapid production of content that appears knowledgeable without necessarily requiring understanding from the user. With its unprecedented ability to rapidly synthesize information from vast datasets, Gen AI can create content that would typically require extensive research and expertise.

While Gen AI can facilitate user understanding by explaining complex information in more digestible formats, some observers worry about the implications of generating knowledge without comprehending its meaning, context, and consequences.

Some thinkers, notably the late great Dr. Henry A. Kissinger, likened the rise of ChatGPT as a major reversal in the progress of human cognitive development. Whereas the invention of the printing press in 1455 accelerated modern human thought, enabling an unprecedented aggregation and dissemination of information step-by-step through the scientific methods of reasoning, Gen AI produces results without explaining how or why. As a result, without our understanding the context

---

[10] Ibid

or meaning of content, he notes, "...our future now holds an entirely novel element of mystery, risk and surprise."[11]

And he does have a point: over-reliance on AI-generated content could lead to a decline in critical thinking and analytical skills. If we all become accustomed to receiving instant, seemingly authoritative answers from AI without engaging in the process of research, analysis, and critical evaluation, it could lead to a world where surface-level knowledge is prioritized over deep understanding.

AI "Groupthink"

One of the more interesting studies in how Gen AI influences human thinking was conducted by two academics in England, who found that a writer's use of generative AI enhances individual creativity but reduces the collective diversity of output.[12]

The researchers asked a group of 293 writers to write a short story, and the content produced by writers who had accessed generative AI were evaluated as more creative, better written, and more enjoyable, than those who did not. However, the generative AI-supported stories are more similar to each other than stories by the non-AI-assisted writers.[13]

They concluded that while writers are better off using Gen AI, less individually novel content is produced – an increase in individual creativity at the cost of diversity of style and topics.[14]

---

[11] "ChatGPT Heralds an Intellectual Revolution," Henry A. Kissinger, Eric Schmidt, and Daniel Huttenlocher, WSJ, February 24, 2023 https://www.henryakissinger.com/articles/chatgpt-heralds-an-intellectual-revolution/

[12] Doshi, Anil R., and Oliver P. Hauser. Generative artificial intelligence enhances individual creativity but reduces the collective diversity of novel content. No. 2312.00506. 2023

[13] Ibid

[14] Ibid

The Boston Consulting Group experiment discussed in the previous chapter found this same result; one might call it "AI Groupthink," (Groupthink defined as the tendency of groups to favor consensus and uniformity of opinion over logic and rationality to avoid conflicting viewpoints).[15]

In the study that measured the performance of the professional services firms' 750 BCG consultants found that while 90% of the participants improved their performance improvement in ideation and content creation, "Our study shows that the technology's relatively uniform output can reduce a group's diversity of thought by 41%."[16]

Manipulation and Disinformation

On a related note, one of the most significant risks is the potential for the creation and rapid spread of misinformation – either by user design or by system hallucination.

A prime example of intentional deception is the phenomenon of "deep fakes" – highly realistic but fabricated video or audio content to manipulate public opinion.

In 2018, a deep fake video of former US President Barack Obama went viral, showing him seemingly insulting then-President Donald Trump. The video, created by filmmaker Jordan Peele to raise awareness about deep fakes, demonstrated how easily such technology could be used to spread misinformation or manipulate public opinion.[17]

---

[15] "What Is Groupthink? Definition, Characteristics, and Causes," Will Kenton, Investopedia, June 12, 2024 https://www.investopedia.com/terms/g/groupthink.asp

[16] Candelon, Francois, Lisa Krayer, Saran Rajendran, and David Zuluaga Martinez. "How People Can Create–and Destroy–Value with Generative AI." BCG Global 21 (2023)

[17] https://www.youtube.com/watch?v=cQ54GDm1eLO

More recently, in 2023, a deep fake video of Ukraine's President Volodymyr Zelensky appearing to call for surrender circulated widely, causing momentary panic before it was debunked.[18]

The potential for deep fakes to influence elections, damage reputations, or even incite violence is a growing concern. Without the ability to critically evaluate the authenticity of such content, individuals and society as a whole become vulnerable to manipulation.

Scammers have used deep fakes of the rich and famous, such as Elon Musk, to endorse seemingly legitimate investment opportunities.[19]

And it's not just the faces and voices of celebrities that are being mimicked. Fraudsters have used deep fakes of senior financial officers of banks to convince bank employees to transfer funds to them.[20]

Given the ease and low cost of such tools, Deloitte's Center for Financial Services predicts that Gen AI-enabled frauds in the United States will reach $40 billion by 2027.[21]

To raise awareness of this risk, members of the board of directors at a major bank holding company were treated to a special teleconference call with the CEO on the company's strategy. Except it wasn't the CEO, but a voice of an AI model, training on the voice of the CEO from prior quarterly earnings calls.[22]

---

[18] https://www.youtube.com/watch?v=X17yrEV5sl4

[19] How "Deepfake Elon Musk" Became the Internet's Biggest Scammer, Stuart A. Thompson, New York Times Aug. 14, 2024 https://www.nytimes.com/interactive/2024/08/14/technology/elon-musk-ai-deepfake-scam.html

[20] Generative AI is expected to magnify the risk of deepfakes and other fraud in banking, Deloitte Center for Financial Services, May 29, 2024 https://www2.deloitte.com/xe/en/insights/industry/financial-services/financial-services-industry-predictions.html#generative-ai-is-expected-to

[21] Ibid

[22] Why AI Risks Are Keeping Board Members Up at Night, Emily Glazer, Wall Street Journal, August 14, 2024 https://www.wsj.com/business/c-suite/ai-risk-management-boardroom-b8956c61?mod=hp_lead_pos11

As we've discussed, generative AI can produce content that appears credible and authoritative, even when it's based on flawed or biased data. Without a deep understanding of the subject matter, users may struggle to distinguish between accurate information and AI-generated falsehoods.

Plagiarism

Another significant risk is the potential for inadvertent copyright violations and plagiarism. Generative AI models are trained on vast amounts of data, including copyrighted material. When generating content, these models may reproduce or closely mimic existing works without attribution.

For instance, in 2022, Getty Images banned the upload and sale of illustrations generated by AI art tools, citing unresolved copyright issues. They later filed a lawsuit against Stability AI, the creator of image-generating AI tool Stable Diffusion, alleging that the company copied and processed millions of images protected by copyright without obtaining the proper licenses.[23]

In the realm of text generation, there have been instances of AI-generated content closely mimicking the style and content of existing works. In 2019, OpenAI initially decided not to release their GPT-2 language model due to concerns about its potential misuse for generating convincing fake news articles. While they later released the model, the incident highlighted the potential for AI to be used for large-scale plagiarism or the creation of misleading content.[24]

---

[23] "Photo giant Getty took a leading AI image-maker to court. Now it's also embracing the technology," Matt O'Brien, Associated Press, September 25, 2023 `https://apnews.com/article/getty-images-artificial-intelligence-ai-image-generator-stable-diffusion-a98eeaaeb2bf13c5e8874ceb6a8ce196`

[24] "OpenAI built a text generator so good, it's considered too dangerous to release," Zack Whittaker,

TechCrunch, February 17, 2019 `https://techcrunch.com/2019/02/17/openai-text-generator-dangerous/`

The risk of plagiarism extends to academic and professional settings as well. As AI-generated essays and reports become more sophisticated, there's a growing concern about students and professionals using these tools to produce work without developing the underlying understanding or skills. This not only raises ethical issues but also potentially undermines the educational process and professional development.

So while generative AI offers tremendous potential benefits, the risks associated with generating knowledge without comprehension are significant and multifaceted. From the spread of misinformation and deep fakes to copyright violations, plagiarism, and the potential erosion of critical thinking skills, these risks underscore the importance of developing AI literacy, implementing robust verification processes, and maintaining a balance between AI assistance and human judgment. As we continue to advance and integrate these technologies, it's crucial that we also develop strategies to mitigate these risks and ensure that AI serves as a tool to enhance, rather than replace, human understanding and critical thinking.

Upsides

Now we turn to the upsides.

Even at the time of this writing, with only some notable exceptions, Gen AI is still in its early, experimental phases. As skeptics have pointed out, there's no clear "killer app" for Gen AI that makes it indispensable or indisputably superior to other products.

The success stories, as impressive as many are, seem to be isolated, partial, and/or idiosyncratic – not systemic or industry-changing. As a group, they seem to be about the widespread potential of the technology – not revolutionary improvements. We still seem to be "playing around" with it; it has yet to go mainstream – become a fixture in our lives as the Internet or smart phones. Perhaps a lot of the buzz about Gen AI in the workplace today is like teenage sex: the volume of talk greatly exceeds the number of actual cases.

In a recent survey of 1,100 global executives by consulting giant Cap Gemini, organizations reported an average increase of 8.1% to productivity, 6.3% to operational efficiency, and 6.2% to customer engagement and satisfaction from their use of Gen AI. Companies also noted a 4.2% rise in sales and a 3.1% decrease in costs.[25]

Sounds impressive, right? But note this: nearly all (98%) of the participants in the survey reported that their organization uses generative AI in some capacity, but may not be getting the full benefits due to the limitations of their infrastructure, data, or budget. [26]

"Some capacity" being the operating term here.

Despite its many drawbacks, we feel that this new wave holds incredible potential to transform our lives.

To those who dismiss Gen AI as merely accessing, retrieving, summarizing, repurposing, integrating, synthesizing material already created, one must ask: isn't that what most of us "knowledge workers" most of the day, hunched over at our desks, staring at our screens, reading, listening to, and watching content – and responding, typing away on our keyboards?

And Gen AI performs these kinds of tasks in seconds – not minutes, hours, days, weeks, or months, as some types of knowledge work take us humans now.

Our key message is this regard: please don't be so quick to dismiss its potential to transform our economy and society. To judge it right now is like dismissing the career prospects of a three-month old. The movement is still in its infancy.[27]

---

[25] Generative AI in Organizations 2024, Cap Gemini Research Institute https://www.capgemini.com/insights/research-library/generative-ai-in-organizations-2024/

[26] Ibid

[27] For the novice user, there are a variety of guides to use Chat PT; a good example is Chat GPT Guide https://www.chatgptguide.ai/all-our-chatgpt-guides/

Inflection Point: Preparing for the Next Big Thing

Now the reader should be reminded that the author – an academic in Data Science specializing in organizational behavior – is not remotely qualified to speculate where the Gen AI revolution is headed. But here goes anyway.

Based on current trends, there are probably quite of few potential inflection points, but one that comes to mind: if/when Gen AI makes a major breakthrough in pharmaceuticals and/or medical diagnostics.

Consider these data points:

- AstraZeneca's Generative AI models are expediting the drug discovery process. By training on vast chemical databases, these models can generate novel molecular structures with desired properties, significantly reducing the time to identify potential drug candidates and potentially accelerating the development of medications.[28]

- Novartis employs generative AI to optimize patient selection for clinical trials, analyzing patient data to generate profiles of ideal candidates to improve drug trial efficiency and outcomes. [29]

---

[28] "Data Science & Artificial Intelligence: Unlocking new science insights," https://www.astrazeneca.com/r-d/data-science-and-ai.html

[29] "Novartis empowers scientists with AI to speed the discovery and development of breakthrough medicines," Bill Briggs, Microsoft, November 18, 2021 https://news.microsoft.com/source/features/digital-transformation/novartis-empowers-scientists-ai-speed-discovery-development-breakthrough-medicines/

- In the field of medical diagnostics, Siemens has integrated generative AI into its medical imaging systems that can produce high-quality images from lower-quality scans, potentially reducing radiation exposure and improving diagnostic accuracy.[30]

- DeepMind's AlphaFold project has demonstrated improved accuracy in predicting protein structures, a crucial step in understanding diseases and developing new treatments. [31]

If any one of these initiatives results in a major breakthrough – a blockbuster, life-saving drug, or treatment – Gen AI technology could well start transforming nearly every endeavor that involves generating content and/or shifting through large amounts of information to create an optimal solution: be it commerce or industry.

A Final Word on Leadership

As we've noted, this book is really meant to be a leadership guide, and as such, we feel compelled to add this observation. When all is said and done, it seems that successful leadership in the age of intelligent machines comes down to three core ingredients:

> Technical Competency (not necessarily expertise):
> The ability to make sound decisions about strategy
> and execution – authentically and clearly.

---

[30] "Siemens Healthineers shows Potential of Generative AI in Medical," November 26, 2023 https://www.siemens-healthineers.com/press/releases/generativeai

[31] "AlphaFold is accelerating research in nearly every field of biology." Google DeepMind https://deepmind.google/technologies/alphafold/

> Common Sense: Understanding the need to have
> specific use cases and a sound technical road map,
> with a detailed business case in terms of return on
> investment (the cautionary tale from that global
> banking head of AI in Chapter 4 comes to mind),
> and lastly, and perhaps counter intuitively.

> Social Intelligence, or "people skills."

That is, for all the blather about Agentic AI, mixture of expert models, compound models, vector stores and embeddings, variational autoencoders, and selective state-based models – leadership is still about dealing with people.

In our chapter on leadership, we discussed the dangers of imposter syndrome. We now cite a recent research study by a Yale management professor and her collaborator at the University of Michigan, who concluded that true success at leadership is how you make others feel, or "positive relational energy," counts the most.

From their empirical analysis, the researchers found that the single strongest predictor is not "...charisma, influence, or power. It is not personality, attractiveness, or innovative genius. The one thing that supersedes all these factors is positive relational energy: the energy exchanged between people that helps uplift, enthuse, and renew them."[32]

Our point here: businesses are not simply arrangements of people, process, and technology; they're not, despite what they appear, exclusively economic systems. First and foremost, they are social organisms.

---

[32] "The Best Leaders Have a Contagious Positive Energy," Emma Seppälä and Kim Cameron, Harvard Business Review, April 18, 2022 https://hbr.org/2022/04/the-best-leaders-have-a-contagious-positive-energy

As a recent *WSJ* columnist put it: "It's about fostering connection and making our conversation partners feel they're the charming—or interesting or funny—ones."[33]

And that leadership style – to embody authentic confidence in, and kindness to, others – seems like a pretty good idea to us, or as some researchers at the University of Oxford conclude: "Indeed, in a world where AI excels in the virtual space, the art of performing in-person will be a particularly valuable skill across a host of managerial, professional and customer-facing occupations. People who can make their presence felt in a room, that have the capacity to forge relationships, to motivate, and to convince, are the people that will thrive in the age of AI."[34]

Bottom Line: The Pre-flight Checklist

And now a final word on organizational transformation: "The Pre-flight Checklist."

You've read that the Productivity Revolution or Industry 4.0 is an evolutionary stage of the previous digital revolution, and it portends major changes in how we work and live – but notably doesn't alter basic principles of running a profitable business and common sense.

And this book argues that this revolution requires new types of roles, functions, and reporting hierarchies that most organizations don't have now, and institutional pressures – from industry competitors, legislators, regulators, Wall Street, academia, and the general public – will continue to mount on businesses to adopt.

---

[33] "Is 'Rizz' the Secret to Getting Ahead at Work?" Rachel Feintzeig, WSJ, July 21, 2024 https://www.wsj.com/lifestyle/workplace/what-is-rizz-how-to-work-tips-50787508?mod=wknd_pos1

[34] Frey, Carl Benedikt, and Michael Osborne. "Generative AI and the future of work: a reappraisal." Brown Journal of World Affairs 30, no. 1 (2024), p. 3

At this point, you probably have three big questions, mainly

1. What can I use these things for? What types of models can I apply in my business processes to make things faster, cheaper, better and/or give me a competitive advantage?

2. How do avoid creating problems? What do I need to do to ensure things go right?

3. What's the ROI or breakeven? How much will this cost my organization, relative to the benefits?

To this end, we offer a "pre-flight checklist" for those managers feeling a bit overwhelmed about the excitement and buzz, and with a healthy skepticism earned from surviving previous management fads that involved undertaking journeys without specific details on the destinations.

That is, before asking your team to develop that RFP to present to the executive committee and the board of directors on a multi-million-dollar proposal to infuse AI into your organization, ask yourself these five simple sets of questions:

1. Data and Infrastructure: Is the data governance and data management infrastructure of sufficient maturity and readiness? Are internal proprietary datasets of sufficient quality and discoverability to be securely used to fine-tune/augment LLMs? Is the computing infrastructure robust and secure enough to handle the data computational volume and performance requirements of Gen AI?

2. Talent: Do you have the talent (internally or outsourced) to help you decide whether and to what extent your organization can honestly, realistically, and accurately assess the feasibility and applicability of many different variants of LLMs in the marketplace in your business model?

Note   You don't need AI experts, but you need data scientists with sufficient understanding of the LLM ecosystem and what capabilities come with what costs.

3. Use Cases: Do you understand the potential applications of these technologies in your business processes? What is the value-add or competitive advantage to be gained, at what cost? Do you have specific use cases for which you can develop a proof-of-concept or prototype? Do you have clear performance and cost-benefit metrics by which to make these judgments?

Note   As a general rule, if your use cases don't involve creating content and are about analyzing vast amounts of data to identify, classify, or predict some outcome, perhaps a machine algorithm or neural net package from an open source neural network library or exchange will prove to be a much cheaper and easier to implement solution than an LLM.

Also note: if you're just starting on this journey, don't worry about having a "strategic vision for organizational transformation to your target operating model" or other such nonsense as a prerequisite.

If all goes well on the initial adoption phases of these technologies, you will have the luxury of having that problem to solve down the road – but not now.

4. Governance, Risk, and Compliance: Are roles and responsibilities clearly defined, and is there sufficient transparency in performance monitoring as to who is accountable for what? Do you have detailed, specific milestones, deliverables, and budget tracking? Do you have the organizational capacity to assess, monitor, and ensure the risks the firm takes are worth their expected returns – the tools, metrics, and processes to measure upside opportunity relative to downside risk?

   Also, do you have a culture of compliance, the right "tone at the top"? Do you have sufficient resources and capabilities to identify, risk-rate, and design and test controls on highly risk-rated financial, operational, regulatory, and reputational risks? Are there processes, controls, and tests of those controls in place to manage the risks of transparency, data security, fairness and bias recognition, accountability, legal, and ethical considerations?

   And lastly, and perhaps most importantly...

5. Leadership: Do you have the executive support and organizational buy-in to adopt these new technologies? Does the culture encourage open and honest communication that supports teamwork, collaboration, and matrix management, or does getting different political fiefdoms to cooperate and

share information and resources feel like pulling teeth? Are functions such as employee education, change management, and continuous learning ongoing processes or special, one-off occasions? Does management support a culture of innovation, experimentation, continuous improvement, and learning from mistakes (i.e., are people allowed to fail?).

If you get at least most of those right, you stand a very good chance of succeeding.

APPENDIX A

Data Governance Best Practices

This appendix goes into more detail on best practices in Data Governance.

Data Quality Metrics

Another important component to Data Governance is the use of metrics to evaluate data quality over time and compare the quality of different data sources to gain insights into the reliability, accuracy, completeness, and consistency of their data assets. Here's why and how organizations utilize metrics for evaluating data quality and prioritizing remediation efforts:

- Understanding Data Quality Trends: By tracking data quality metrics over time, organizations can identify trends, patterns, and anomalies in data quality performance. Monitoring metrics such as data accuracy, completeness, consistency, timeliness, and integrity allows organizations to assess how data quality evolves and fluctuates over different time periods. For example, organizations may observe seasonal variations in data quality, periodic spikes or dips in data accuracy, or long-term trends indicating gradual degradation or improvement in data quality. These insights help organizations understand the factors influencing data quality and prioritize remediation efforts accordingly.

© Arthur J. O'Connor 2024
A. J. O'Connor, *Organizing for Generative AI and the Productivity Revolution*,
https://doi.org/10.1007/979-8-8688-0959-0

- Benchmarking Data Sources: Metrics enable organizations to compare the quality of different data sources, systems, or processes against predefined benchmarks or industry standards. By establishing baseline metrics and performance targets, organizations can assess the relative quality of data from various sources and identify outliers or underperforming datasets. For instance, organizations may compare data quality metrics such as error rates, completeness percentages, or duplication rates across multiple data sources or systems. This comparative analysis helps administrators pinpoint areas of concern and allocate resources effectively to improve data quality where it is most needed.

- Identifying Data Quality Issues: Data quality metrics serve as diagnostic tools for identifying specific data quality issues, errors, or anomalies within datasets. Metrics provide quantitative insights into the nature and extent of data quality problems, enabling administrators to diagnose root causes and take corrective actions. For example, anomalies in data consistency metrics may indicate discrepancies or conflicts between data sources, while low completeness metrics may suggest missing or incomplete data records. By analyzing these metrics, administrators can prioritize remediation efforts and implement targeted interventions to address underlying data quality issues.

- Prioritizing Remediation Efforts: Metrics help organizations prioritize remediation efforts by quantifying the impact and severity of data quality issues and assessing their business implications. Administrators can use metrics to prioritize remediation based on factors such as data criticality, business impact, regulatory compliance requirements, and stakeholder priorities. For instance, high-impact data quality issues affecting mission-critical systems or regulatory reporting may be prioritized over lower-priority issues with minimal business impact. By aligning remediation efforts with strategic objectives and business priorities, organizations can optimize resource allocation and maximize the return on investment in data quality improvement initiatives.

- Driving Continuous Improvement: Data quality metrics support a culture of continuous improvement by providing feedback loops and performance benchmarks for monitoring progress and driving accountability. Organizations can use metrics to set goals, track performance against targets, and measure the effectiveness of data quality initiatives over time.

By establishing key performance indicators (KPIs) and monitoring progress against these metrics, organizations can identify areas for improvement, celebrate successes, and identify opportunities for further optimization.

This iterative approach to data quality management fosters a culture of data-driven decision-making and continuous improvement across the organization.

What's Different About Data Governance with Generative AI?

As organizations increasingly integrate LLMs into their operations to drive innovation, the importance of Data Governance grows exponentially – and not just because generative AI relies heavily on access to vast amounts of data, including internal proprietary data, to train and refine models.

Why the escalation in importance? We can think of three main reasons:

1. In addition to the established concerns of data integrity, compliance with data privacy regulations, and data security to prevent unauthorized access, there come new challenges in mitigating bias in training data and interpretable and responsible AI (we'll get into this topic in the next chapter).

2. New types of data models combining structured with unstructured[1] data and new distributed data architectures require new strategies and approaches to data and metadata management.

3. Data flows in the petabyte (or millions of millions of bytes) scale require new and automated data acquisition and management architectures, as the current state of fragmented approaches and manual interventions across different data fiefdoms becomes impossible to manage.

---

[1] We find the term "unstructured data" a bit misleading, as it refers to data that doesn't fit neatly into a structured database format: things like text, images, videos, or audio recordings. While the data may seem chaotic, much "unstructured" data actually possesses underlying structure or patterns that can be discovered and utilized.

These data pipelines sometimes require extensive cleaning, missing data imputation, and munging (process of converting raw data into a more usable format) to normalize the data in a standardized format across the enterprise.

But perhaps the biggest reason is that, for most organizations, the stakes (risks and rewards) are so much higher.

In the past, when most data was used for offline decision-support and reporting, most organizations could get by with "good enough" quality data. But "good enough" data is potentially disastrous when the results of data are used to make important decisions and drive mission-critical business processes like order fulfillment, supply chain optimization, quality control, or customer service – and/or when organizations sell their generated data to third parties, based on the promise of accuracy and efficacy.

Just consider the operational and reputational risk of hallucinations – false or misleading information presented as fact.

For the purposes of this chapter, we'll discuss a broad range of requirements, from new strategies and architectures for managing data and metadata, as well as the need for upgrading current practices.

Mitigating Bias in Training Data

A major concern and challenge in generative AI is migrating the risk of bias in training data. In essence: models trained on data reflecting biases will produce those same biases. Some strategies to consider:

Diverse Data Collection

- Ensure that your training dataset represents a wide range of demographics, backgrounds, and perspectives.

- Avoid underrepresentation: Pay attention to minority groups or less-represented classes to prevent bias.

Automated Preprocessing

- Instead of simple quality checks for missing values, misclassified fields, violation of data types, and formats, use machine learning classification models to identify biases in your data, such as:

  - Balance class distribution: Oversample underrepresented classes or under-sampled overrepresented ones.

  - Remove irrelevant features: Eliminate features that introduce bias or are not relevant to the task.

Annotation Guidelines

- Clear guidelines: Provide annotators with explicit instructions on labeling data.

- Address potential biases: Highlight potential pitfalls related to bias during annotation.

Fair Sampling

- Stratified sampling: Ensure that each subgroup is well-represented in your training data.

- Adaptive sampling: Adjust sampling based on model performance to reduce bias.

Regularization Techniques

- Weighted loss functions: Assign different weights to different classes to balance their impact.

- Fairness-aware regularization: Penalize models for making biased predictions.

De-biasing Algorithms

- Adversarial training: Train a model to predict the protected attribute (e.g., gender) and minimize its influence on the main task.

- Reweighting instances: Adjust instance weights to reduce bias.

Post-processing

- Calibration: Adjust model predictions to ensure fairness across different groups.

- Threshold tuning: Set decision thresholds based on fairness considerations.

Evaluate Fairness Metrics

- Demographic parity: Compare outcomes across different groups.

- Equalized odds: Assess whether false positives/ negatives are balanced across groups.

- Disparate impact: Measure bias in decision outcomes.

Human Oversight and Intervention

- Review and iterate: Continuously assess model performance and address biases.

- Feedback from diverse stakeholders: Involve people from different backgrounds to provide insights.

Transparency and Documentation

- Document data collection and preprocessing: Maintain a record of decisions made during data preparation.

- Explainable AI: Use interpretable models to understand how decisions are made.

Retrieval Augmented Generation

One of the key advancements in AI techniques that has heightened the significance of Data Governance is Retrieval Augmented Generation (RAG). RAG combines retrieval-based methods with generative models to improve the relevance and coherence of generated outputs. While this technique enhances the capabilities of AI systems by enabling them to retrieve and synthesize information from vast repositories of data, it also introduces new challenges for Data Governance. Specifically, RAG necessitates careful management of the data used for retrieval to ensure its accuracy, relevance, and compliance with regulations and organizational policies.

This integration of proprietary data into AI systems enables organizations to create new business models, products, services, and processes that leverage the insights derived from this data-driven approach. However, with this integration comes the need for robust Data Governance practices to ensure the ethical, legal, and responsible use of data.

Access Controls

In the context of large language models (LLMs) and other AI systems, the principle of least privilege is equally important, albeit with some unique considerations. But for the principle to be effectively implemented with LLMs, an organization needs to adopt a more automated and streamlined process for creating, modifying, editing, and deleting user profiles and permission levels.

Again, we return to the theme that current best practices in Data Governance have become basic requirements in the age of LLMs.

In terms of security user profiles, it's a matter of not what, but how access controls should be implemented to ensure that only authorized personnel have access to the data used to train and fine-tune LLMs. This involves User Access Management Systems to house, maintain, and update roles and permissions based on job functions and responsibilities, to ensure access is granted only to those individuals who require it to perform

180

their tasks effectively. Additionally, data encryption and anonymization techniques may be employed to further protect sensitive information and limit exposure to unauthorized users.

During the deployment and operation of LLMs, access controls should also be enforced to restrict interactions with the model to authorized applications and processes. This helps prevent malicious actors from exploiting vulnerabilities in the AI system to gain unauthorized access or manipulate its behavior. Access controls can include mechanisms such as authentication, authorization, and audit trails to monitor and control access to LLMs and the data they process.

Furthermore, the principle of least privilege extends beyond data access to encompass other aspects of LLM design and implementation, such as model architecture, APIs, and deployment environments. For example, developers should adhere to the principle of least privilege when designing APIs for interacting with LLMs, ensuring that only essential functionalities are exposed and that access is granted based on the principle of least privilege.

Moving to the topic of data management, we turn to workflow automation, knowledge graphs, heterogeneous data architectures, and other important components to effective Data Governance.

Workflow Automation

Workflow automation plays a crucial role in orchestrating complex data pipelines for data cleansing, transformation, and enrichment, enabling organizations to manage a higher number of workloads efficiently and effectively. Here's how workflow automation technologies facilitate the development of organized and repeatable data pipelines for provisioning numerous analytics and AI/ML workloads:

Orchestration of Interdependent Processes: Workflow automation platforms allow organizations to define and orchestrate interdependent processes within data pipelines, ensuring that data cleansing, transformation, and enrichment tasks are executed in a coordinated and sequential manner.

181

For example, a workflow may include tasks such as data ingestion, quality checks, schema validation, transformation logic execution, enrichment with external data sources, and data loading into target systems – and of course normalization if data sources are heterogeneous. Workflow automation ensures that each task is executed in the correct sequence and that dependencies between tasks are managed effectively.

Parallel Execution of Workloads: Workflow automation technologies enable organizations to parallelize the execution of workloads within data pipelines, allowing multiple tasks to be processed concurrently to improve overall throughput and performance.

For instance, data cleansing, transformation, and enrichment tasks can be divided into smaller units of work and distributed across multiple processing nodes or clusters for parallel execution. This parallelization strategy accelerates data processing and reduces time-to-insight for analytics and AI/ML workloads.

Error Handling and Retry Mechanisms: Workflow automation platforms incorporate error handling and retry mechanisms to handle failures and exceptions gracefully during data pipeline execution. Automated workflows can detect errors, retry failed tasks, and escalate unresolved issues to designated stakeholders for resolution.

For example, if a data transformation task encounters an error due to missing data or invalid values, the workflow automation system can automatically retry the task a predefined number of times or trigger an alert to notify data stewards or administrators for intervention.

Dynamic Workflow Orchestration: Workflow automation technologies support dynamic workflow orchestration, allowing organizations to adapt data pipelines dynamically based on changing data, business rules, or environmental conditions.

For instance, workflows can be configured to scale up or down dynamically in response to fluctuations in data volumes, processing demands, or resource availability. This elasticity ensures optimal resource utilization and performance for data pipelines.

Reusable Workflow Templates and Components: Workflow automation platforms enable organizations to create reusable templates and components for common data cleansing, transformation, and enrichment tasks, accelerating pipeline development and promoting consistency and standardization.

Organizations can develop a library of predefined workflow templates, task templates, and transformation logic components that can be easily reused and customized for different analytics and AI/ML workloads. This reusability reduces development time and effort and ensures consistency across data pipelines.

Integration with Analytics and AI/ML Tools: Workflow automation technologies seamlessly integrate with analytics and AI/ML tools, enabling organizations to orchestrate end-to-end data pipelines that encompass data preparation, model training, evaluation, and deployment.

For example, workflows can be designed to automate the entire machine learning lifecycle, from data ingestion and feature engineering to model training, hyper-parameter tuning, and model deployment.

Workflow automation ensures that data pipelines are orchestrated in a structured, repeatable, and scalable manner, regardless of the complexity of the underlying processes or the number of workloads involved. By leveraging workflow automation technologies, organizations can streamline data pipeline development, optimize resource utilization, and accelerate time-to-insight for analytics and AI/ML initiatives, ultimately driving greater business value and competitive advantage. The benefits are

Speed and Efficiency

- Automation accelerates the data preparation process by eliminating manual interventions and streamlining repetitive tasks. Automated workflows can handle data acquisition, transformation, integration, cleansing, and enrichment at scale and with greater speed compared to manual processes.

- By automating routine data preparation tasks, organizations can reduce processing times, minimize delays, and improve overall operational efficiency. This allows data to be made available for analysis, reporting, and decision-making in a timely manner, enabling faster insights and action.

Consistency and Accuracy

- Automated data preparation ensures consistency and accuracy by applying predefined rules, standards, and transformations consistently across all data sources and records. Manual processes are prone to human errors, inconsistencies, and variations, leading to data quality issues and unreliable results.

- Automation reduces the risk of errors, discrepancies, and data inconsistencies by enforcing data quality checks, validation rules, and reconciliation mechanisms throughout the data preparation pipeline. This improves data integrity and reliability, enhancing trust in the resulting insights and decisions.

Scalability and Flexibility

- Automated data preparation is highly scalable and adaptable to changing data volumes, sources, and requirements. Automated workflows can handle large volumes of data and accommodate diverse data formats, structures, and sources without manual intervention.

- Automation enables organizations to scale their data preparation processes seamlessly as data volumes grow or new data sources are introduced. This scalability ensures that data pipelines can handle increasing workloads and complexity without sacrificing performance or efficiency.

Resource Optimization

- Automation optimizes resource utilization by freeing up human resources from manual data preparation tasks to focus on higher-value activities such as data analysis, interpretation, and decision-making. This allows organizations to make better use of skilled personnel and expertise, maximizing productivity and innovation.

- By automating repetitive and mundane data preparation tasks, organizations can reduce labor costs, minimize operational overhead, and reallocate resources to strategic initiatives that drive business value and competitive advantage.

Agility and Responsiveness

- Automated data preparation enables organizations to respond quickly to changing business needs, market dynamics, and regulatory requirements. Automated workflows can be easily modified, extended, or reconfigured to accommodate new data sources, transformations, or business rules.

- Automation promotes agility and responsiveness in data management, allowing organizations to adapt to evolving data landscapes, technology trends, and competitive pressures with greater speed and agility. This agility enables organizations to stay ahead of the curve and capitalize on emerging opportunities more effectively.

Role of Data Catalogs in Automating Pipelines

Data catalogs play a crucial role in improving the efficiency, reliability, and governance of data pipelines by providing a centralized repository of metadata and facilitating data discovery, lineage tracking, and collaboration among stakeholders. Here's how data catalogs can enhance the effectiveness of data pipelines:

Rapid Data Discovery

- Data catalogs enable rapid data discovery by providing a centralized inventory of available data assets, including structured, semi-structured, and unstructured data. Pipeline developers can quickly search and browse the catalog to identify relevant datasets, schemas, and data sources for their pipelines.

- Metadata stored in the catalog, such as data descriptions, tags, and annotations, help developers understand the content, structure, and usage patterns of different datasets, allowing them to make informed decisions about data selection and integration in their pipelines.

- By streamlining the data discovery process, data catalogs reduce the time and effort required to locate and onboard data into pipelines, accelerating pipeline development and deployment cycles.

Guidance on Trusted and Governed Data

- Data catalogs provide guidance to pipeline developers on using trusted and governed data assets wherever possible. Trusted data assets are those that have undergone quality assurance, validation, and compliance checks, ensuring their reliability, accuracy, and compliance with organizational policies and standards.

- Metadata in the catalog can include quality metrics, lineage information, access controls, and data governance policies associated with each data asset. Pipeline developers can use this information to assess the trustworthiness and suitability of data for their pipelines and make informed decisions about data usage.

- By promoting the use of trusted and governed data, data catalogs help ensure data integrity, consistency, and compliance throughout the data pipeline lifecycle, reducing the risk of errors, inconsistencies, and regulatory issues.

Crowdsourced Knowledge Sharing

- Some advanced data catalogs incorporate crowdsourcing functionality that allows users to contribute annotations, ratings, reviews, and feedback about data assets. This crowdsourced knowledge provides valuable insights, context, and user experiences that can help pipeline developers better understand and evaluate less-well-known datasets.

- Crowdsourced metadata annotations can include user-generated tags, descriptions, usage patterns, and recommendations for specific data assets. Pipeline developers can leverage this collective intelligence to assess the relevance, quality, and reliability of datasets and make more informed decisions about their inclusion in pipelines.

- By tapping into crowdsourced knowledge, data catalogs foster collaboration, knowledge sharing, and community-driven curation of data assets, enriching the metadata ecosystem and enhancing data discovery and usage across the organization.

Centralized vs. Decentralized vs. Federated Metadata Management

Creating a centralized and trusted collection of metadata is crucial for enabling users, developers, and automated applications to understand and effectively utilize data from various sources. Different strategies (Centralized, Distributed, and Federated) exist for achieving this goal, each with its own set of advantages and disadvantages:

Centralized Metadata Repository

Advantages

- Centralizing metadata in a single repository provides a unified view of data assets across the organization, promoting consistency and standardization in data management practices.

- Users and developers can easily access and search for metadata from a centralized location, streamlining data discovery and enhancing productivity.

- Centralized metadata repositories often include features for data governance, such as data lineage tracking, data quality metrics, and access controls, ensuring data integrity and compliance with regulations.

Disadvantages

- Building and maintaining a centralized metadata repository can be resource-intensive and require significant upfront investment in infrastructure, tools, and governance processes.

- Ensuring the accuracy and completeness of metadata in a centralized repository can be challenging, especially when integrating data from disparate sources with varying formats and quality.

- Dependency on a single repository creates a potential single point of failure, increasing the risk of data loss or downtime if the repository experiences issues.

Distributed Metadata Management

Advantages

- Distributed metadata management allows metadata to be stored alongside the data it describes, reducing latency and improving data accessibility for users and applications.

- Each data source or system maintains its own metadata, which can be tailored to specific requirements and preferences, providing flexibility and autonomy for data owners.

- Distributed metadata management minimizes the risk of data inconsistency or synchronization issues that may arise in centralized repositories, as metadata is closely tied to the data it describes.

Disadvantages

- Managing metadata across distributed systems can lead to fragmentation and duplication of metadata, making it challenging to maintain a comprehensive and consistent view of data assets.

- Discoverability and accessibility of metadata may vary between different data sources and systems, requiring users to navigate multiple interfaces and formats to access relevant information.

- Lack of centralized governance and standardization in distributed metadata management can result in inconsistencies, inaccuracies, and conflicts in metadata definitions and structures.

Federated Metadata Catalogs

Advantages

- Federated metadata catalogs integrate metadata from multiple sources and systems into a unified catalog, providing users with a centralized view of data assets while leveraging distributed metadata management capabilities.

- Users can search and discover metadata across different data sources and systems through a single interface, improving efficiency and usability.

- Federated metadata catalogs promote collaboration and interoperability between disparate data management systems, enabling organizations to leverage existing investments and technologies.

Disadvantages

- Integrating metadata from heterogeneous sources and systems into a federated catalog requires careful planning and coordination to ensure compatibility, consistency, and accuracy.

- Synchronization and alignment of metadata between federated catalogs and underlying data sources may introduce latency and overhead, impacting performance and responsiveness.

- Federated metadata catalogs may face challenges in managing access controls, security policies, and governance requirements across distributed data environments, potentially compromising data privacy and compliance.

New Techniques for Data and Metadata Management

Traditional relational data management, as used in business intelligence (BI) and data warehousing (DW) systems, as well as applications like customer relationship management (CRM), primarily focuses on managing structured data that conforms to predefined schemas, formats, and structures. In these systems, data relationships tend to be relatively simple and limited in number compared to the complex and interconnected relationships found in knowledge graphs and graph databases.

In relational data management systems, data is typically organized into tables with rows and columns, where each table represents a specific entity or aspect of the business. Relationships between data entities are established through foreign key constraints or joins between tables, based on well-defined primary and foreign key relationships. This rigid structure facilitates efficient querying, reporting, and analysis of structured data, making it well-suited for BI and DW systems where the emphasis is on aggregating and analyzing large volumes of structured data to derive insights.

In contrast, knowledge graphs and graph databases offer a more flexible and expressive way to model complex data relationships, including both structured and unstructured data. Unlike relational databases, which rely on predefined schemas, knowledge graphs allow organizations to represent diverse types of data entities and their relationships using nodes and edges. This enables the modeling of rich semantic connections between data elements, facilitating more nuanced analysis and discovery of data relationships.

Organizations leverage knowledge graphs and graph databases as powerful tools to memorialize data relationships across various domains, including data dictionaries, data catalogs, and Master Data Management (MDM) systems. Knowledge graphs represent data entities as nodes and their relationships as edges, providing a flexible and scalable way to model complex data structures and capture rich semantic information. By organizing data in this manner, organizations can gain deeper insights into data relationships, enhance data governance, and facilitate more efficient data discovery and integration processes.

In the context of data dictionaries and data catalogs, knowledge graphs enable organizations to document and visualize the relationships between different data elements, attributes, and schemas. This helps users understand the structure and meaning of data assets, identify dependencies, and navigate data landscapes more effectively. For example, a knowledge graph may represent relationships between database tables, columns, and data types, as well as mappings between different data sources or systems. This holistic view of data relationships enhances data lineage and impact analysis, supporting data governance and compliance initiatives.

Similarly, in Master Data Management (MDM) systems, knowledge graphs play a critical role in managing and reconciling data from disparate sources to create a single, authoritative view of master data entities such as customers, products, or locations. By modeling relationships between master data entities and their attributes, hierarchies, and classifications, organizations can establish a unified data model that facilitates consistent data management and improves data quality. Knowledge graphs enable MDM systems to capture complex relationships between master data entities, such as customer hierarchies, product associations, or geographic dependencies, enabling more accurate and comprehensive data management.

Implicit vs. Explicit Data

One of the key challenges in managing knowledge graphs and graph databases involves mapping relationships between "implicit" behavioral data and "explicit" data.

Implicit data refers to information derived from user interactions, behaviors, or observations, such as website clicks, search queries, or social media engagements. On the other hand, explicit data results from intentional actions or inputs provided by users, such as making a purchase, submitting feedback, or rating a product using a star rating system.

Mapping relationships between implicit and explicit data allows organizations to enrich their knowledge graphs with valuable insights into user behaviors and preferences. For example, organizations can analyze implicit behavioral data to identify patterns, trends, and correlations that inform personalized recommendations, targeted marketing campaigns, or product enhancements. By linking implicit data with explicit actions, such as purchase history or feedback ratings, organizations can create a more holistic view of customer interactions and preferences, enabling more effective decision-making and customer engagement strategies.

Moreover, knowledge graphs are particularly well-suited for capturing and analyzing implicit data, such as user behaviors and interactions, which may not fit neatly into predefined schemas or tables. By modeling implicit data as nodes and edges in a graph structure, organizations can uncover hidden patterns, correlations, and insights that may not be apparent through traditional relational data management approaches.

Furthermore, while relational databases excel at managing structured data with known definitions, formats, and structures, they may struggle to handle unstructured or semi-structured data, such as text documents, social media posts, or multimedia content. In contrast, knowledge graphs and graph databases offer greater flexibility in managing diverse data types and integrating information from disparate sources, making them well-suited for applications requiring a more holistic view of data relationships, such as customer master data files.

Data Lakes vs. Delta Lakes

Storing and managing large amounts of "unstructured" data, along with structured data from less familiar sources and applications, often requires specialized approaches to handle the diverse nature of the data. Two common strategies for managing such data are data lakes and Delta Lake.

Data Lake: Data lakes are centralized repositories that store vast amounts of raw data in its native format, including structured, semi-structured, and unstructured data. Data lakes provide a cost-effective and scalable solution for storing diverse data types without the need for upfront schema design or data transformation. Key characteristics and strategies for managing data lakes include

- Schema-on-read: Unlike traditional databases that enforce a schema upfront, data lakes adopt a schema-on-read approach. Data is ingested into the lake in its raw form, and the schema is applied at the time of data access or analysis. This flexibility allows organizations to store diverse data types without imposing rigid structures.

- Support for diverse data formats: Data lakes support a wide range of data formats, including JSON, Parquet, Avro, CSV, and more. This enables organizations to ingest and store data from various sources and applications without requiring extensive data transformation.

- Scalability: Data lakes are designed to scale horizontally, allowing organizations to store petabytes of data and accommodate growing data volumes over time. Cloud-based data lake solutions, such as Amazon S3, Azure Data Lake Storage, and Google Cloud Storage, offer virtually unlimited storage capacity and on-demand scalability.

- Metadata management: Effective metadata management is essential for governing and cataloging data within the lake. Metadata provides context and lineage information about the stored data, making it easier to discover, understand, and trust the data assets.

Delta Lake: Delta Lake is an open source storage layer that brings ACID (Atomicity, Consistency, Isolation, Durability) transactions to Apache Spark and big data workloads. Delta Lake builds on top of existing data lake infrastructure, such as Apache Hadoop or cloud object stores, to provide reliability, performance, and data management capabilities for big data analytics. Key features and strategies for managing data with Delta Lake include

- Transaction support: Delta Lake provides ACID transactions for data ingestion, updates, deletes, and queries, ensuring data consistency and reliability for complex analytics workloads. This makes it suitable for use cases requiring data consistency and integrity, such as data warehousing and machine learning.

- Schema enforcement and evolution: Delta Lake supports schema enforcement to ensure that ingested data adheres to predefined schemas, preventing data quality issues and inconsistencies. Additionally, it enables schema evolution, allowing schema changes to be applied seamlessly without disrupting existing data pipelines or analytics processes.

- Time travel and versioning: Delta Lake offers time travel capabilities, allowing users to query data snapshots at specific points in time or revert to previous versions of the data. This feature is invaluable for auditing, debugging, and recovering from errors in data pipelines.

- Optimized performance: Delta Lake employs various optimizations, such as file format optimization, data skipping, and caching, to improve query performance and reduce latency for analytical workloads. These optimizations enable organizations to achieve faster query execution and higher throughput for big data processing tasks.

These new forms of distributed data architectures come with distinct advantages and disadvantages when it comes to metadata. Let's compare and contrast three different approaches to managing metadata for data stored in various formats, including semi- and unstructured data:

Centralizing Metadata in a Data Lake
Advantages

- Centralizing metadata in a data lake simplifies data discovery and relationship mapping by providing a unified repository for metadata from diverse data sources and formats.

- Using XML or JSON formats or log files can facilitate the organization and standardization of metadata, making it easier to extract, search, and analyze metadata attributes.

- Centralized metadata in a data lake enables organizations to leverage scalable storage and processing capabilities for managing large volumes of metadata alongside raw data.

Disadvantages

- Managing metadata for semi- and unstructured data in a data lake may require additional effort to extract, transform, and load (ETL) metadata from disparate sources into a consistent format.

- XML or JSON formats may not capture all relevant metadata attributes or relationships for complex data types, limiting the effectiveness of metadata management for certain use cases.

- Centralizing metadata in a data lake may introduce dependencies and performance bottlenecks if metadata operations compete with data processing tasks for resources.

Establishing a Specialized Data Catalog for Analytics Projects

Advantages

- A specialized data catalog tailored to a specific analytics project allows team members to quickly locate relevant data in multiple systems and resolve discrepancies in data definitions, streamlining the data discovery and analysis process.

- By focusing on specific analytics requirements and use cases, a specialized data catalog can provide customized metadata attributes, search capabilities, and integration features optimized for the project's needs.

- Establishing a dedicated data catalog for analytics projects promotes collaboration, knowledge sharing, and alignment among team members, enhancing productivity and decision-making.

Disadvantages

- Creating and maintaining a specialized data catalog requires upfront investment in resources, expertise, and infrastructure, which may not be feasible for every project or organization.

- Specialized data catalogs may lack interoperability and scalability compared to centralized metadata repositories, limiting their usefulness for broader data management initiatives beyond individual projects.

- Customizing metadata attributes and search capabilities for specific analytics projects may introduce complexity and overhead, potentially hindering flexibility and adaptability to evolving requirements.

Setting Up a Cloud-Based Data Catalog with Crowdsourcing Functionality

Advantages

- Leveraging a cloud-based data catalog with crowdsourcing functionality enables organizations to tap into collective knowledge and expertise to enhance metadata quality, completeness, and relevance.

- Integrating crowdsourcing features such as user-contributed annotations, ratings, and feedback allows stakeholders to collaborate in enriching metadata, improving data discoverability and usability.

- Cloud-based data catalogs offer scalability, flexibility, and cost-effectiveness, allowing organizations to leverage cloud platform services and infrastructure for managing metadata across diverse data environments.

Disadvantages

- Implementing crowdsourcing functionality for metadata management requires careful planning, governance, and oversight to ensure data accuracy, security, and compliance with privacy regulations.

- User-contributed metadata annotations and feedback may introduce bias, inconsistencies, or inaccuracies, requiring mechanisms for validation, moderation, and version control.

- Dependence on a specific cloud platform for hosting the data catalog may limit interoperability and portability with other systems or environments, potentially locking organizations into proprietary solutions.

Summary

So, in conclusion, organizations need to start treating Data Governance seriously if they want to productize data and monetize their investments in LLMs. Datasets need to be clean and accurate if they really want to create value – in the form of actionable personalization and customization in the demand chain or efficiency, effectiveness, or speed in the supply chain.

APPENDIX B

12 Pivotal IT Roles in Organizational Transformation

We list 12 roles, providing a summary job description along with responsibilities and skills. Feel free to use these outlines as position descriptions in recruiting such talent.

Depending on your own organization's size and business model, you may not need all 12 functions. These roles are presented to provide an understanding of the key functions and capabilities to support successful adoption of Gen AI.

We start with the role of the data scientist, which has rapidly evolved over recent years from a primarily back office/decision support role to key player in the design and implementation of mission-critical production systems.

Data Scientist

The mission of the data scientist is to leverage data and advanced analytics techniques to solve complex business problems, create value, and drive data-informed decision-making across the organization. This role bridges the gap between business strategy, data analysis, and technological implementation.

© Arthur J. O'Connor 2024
A. J. O'Connor, *Organizing for Generative AI and the Productivity Revolution*,
https://doi.org/10.1007/979-8-8688-0959-0

Key Responsibilities

1. Business Problem Understanding and Framing

    – Collaborate with stakeholders to identify and define key business challenges.

    – Translate business requirements into data science problems.

    – Develop hypotheses and analytical approaches to address business needs.

    – Assess the feasibility and potential impact of data science solutions.

2. Data Collection and Management

    – Identify relevant data sources (internal and external) for analysis.

    – Design data collection strategies when necessary.

    – Collaborate with data engineers to ensure data quality and accessibility.

    – Implement data validation and cleaning processes.

    – Contribute to data governance and documentation efforts.

3. Exploratory Data Analysis (EDA)

    – Perform in-depth exploratory analysis to understand data characteristics.

    – Identify patterns, trends, and anomalies in datasets.

    – Develop visualizations to communicate insights effectively.

    – Generate hypotheses for further investigation.

4. Feature Engineering and Selection

    –   Create meaningful features from raw data to improve model performance.

    –   Apply domain knowledge to develop relevant features.

    –   Implement feature selection techniques to identify the most impactful variables.

    –   Develop automated feature engineering pipelines.

5. Model Development and Evaluation

    –   Design and implement machine learning models (supervised, unsupervised, and reinforcement learning).

    –   Apply statistical techniques for hypothesis testing and inference.

    –   Develop deep learning models for complex problems (e.g., computer vision, NLP).

    –   Implement model evaluation metrics and validation techniques.

    –   Conduct A/B testing to compare model performance.

6. Model Optimization and Tuning

    –   Perform hyper-parameter tuning to optimize model performance.

    –   Implement advanced techniques like ensemble methods and neural architecture search.

    –   Address issues of model bias and fairness.

    –   Optimize models for computational efficiency and scalability.

7. Model Interpretation and Explainability

   – Implement techniques for model interpretability (e.g., SHAP values, LIME).

   – Develop visualizations to explain model decisions to non-technical stakeholders.

   – Address ethical considerations in model development and deployment.

8. Model Deployment and Monitoring

   – Collaborate with ML engineers to deploy models in production environments.

   – Develop monitoring systems to track model performance over time.

   – Implement strategies for model updating and retraining.

   – Contribute to the development of MLOps practices.

9. Data Storytelling and Communication

   – Present findings and recommendations to stakeholders at all levels.

   – Develop clear, concise reports and presentations.

   – Translate complex technical concepts into business language.

   – Create interactive dashboards and data visualizations.

10. Continuous Learning and Innovation

   – Stay current with the latest advancements in data science and machine learning.

   – Experiment with new techniques and technologies.

- Contribute to the data science community through blog posts, talks, or open source projects.

- Mentor junior team members and foster a culture of knowledge sharing.

11. Cross-functional Collaboration

    - Work closely with data engineers, ML engineers, and software developers.

    - Collaborate with domain experts to incorporate subject matter expertise into models.

    - Partner with product managers and business analysts to align data science efforts with strategic goals.

Required Skills and Qualifications

1. Technical Skills

    - Proficiency in programming languages such as Python or R

    - Experience with data manipulation libraries (pandas, dplyr)

    - Familiarity with machine learning frameworks (scikit-learn, TensorFlow, PyTorch)

    - Knowledge of SQL and experience working with databases

    - Understanding of big data technologies (Spark, Hadoop)

    - Experience with version control systems (Git)

    - Familiarity with cloud platforms (AWS, GCP, Azure) and their data science services

2. Mathematical and Statistical Knowledge

   – Strong foundation in statistics and probability theory

   – Understanding of linear algebra and calculus

   – Knowledge of experimental design and causal inference

   – Familiarity with Bayesian methods and probabilistic programming

3. Machine Learning Expertise

   – Deep understanding of classical machine learning algorithms

   – Experience with deep learning architectures and techniques

   – Knowledge of natural language processing and computer vision techniques

   – Understanding of reinforcement learning principles

4. Data Visualization and Communication

   – Proficiency in data visualization tools (Matplotlib, ggplot2, Tableau)

   – Ability to create clear and impactful presentations

   – Strong written and verbal communication skills

5. Business Acumen

   – Understanding of key business metrics and KPIs

   – Ability to translate data insights into actionable business recommendations

   – Knowledge of industry-specific challenges and opportunities

6. Soft Skills

    – Strong problem-solving and analytical thinking

    – Creativity in approaching complex problems

    – Excellent teamwork and collaboration skills

    – Ability to work independently and manage multiple projects

    – Adaptability and willingness to learn new technologies and methods

7. Data Ethics and Governance

    – Understanding of data privacy regulations and ethical considerations

    – Commitment to responsible AI practices

    – Knowledge of model governance and documentation best practices

8. Education and Experience

    – Master's or PhD in Data Science, Computer Science, Statistics, or a related field

    – 3+ years of experience in data science roles

    – Proven track record of delivering impactful data science projects

9. Desirable Certifications

    – Industry-recognized data science certifications (e.g., Google Data Analytics Professional Certificate, IBM Data Science Professional Certificate)

    – Cloud platform certifications (e.g., AWS Certified Machine Learning - Specialty, Google Professional Data Engineer)

207

ML Engineer

The primary objective of the ML engineer is to design, develop, and maintain scalable ML systems that integrate seamlessly with production environments, focusing on the entire ML lifecycle from development to deployment, monitoring, and continuous improvement.

Key Responsibilities

1. ML Model Development and Integration

   – Collaborate with data scientists to translate ML models into production-ready code.

   – Optimize ML algorithms for performance, scalability, and efficiency.

   – Integrate ML models with existing software systems and data pipelines.

   – Implement version control for ML models and associated code.

2. MLOps Infrastructure Design and Implementation

   – Design and build robust MLOps infrastructures to support the entire ML lifecycle.

   – Implement continuous integration and continuous deployment (CI/CD) pipelines for ML models.

   – Set up automated testing frameworks for ML models and systems.

   – Develop reproducible ML workflows and experiments.

3. Model Deployment and Serving

    –   Deploy ML models to production environments
        (cloud, on-premise, or edge devices).

    –   Implement model serving solutions (e.g.,
        TensorFlow Serving, ONNX Runtime).

    –   Optimize model inference for low-latency and
        high-throughput scenarios.

    –   Implement A/B testing frameworks for model
        deployment.

4. Scalability and Performance Optimization

    –   Design and implement distributed computing
        solutions for large-scale ML workloads.

    –   Optimize data processing pipelines for efficiency
        and scalability.

    –   Implement caching and load balancing strategies
        for ML services.

    –   Conduct performance profiling and optimization of
        ML systems.

5. Model Monitoring and Maintenance

    –   Develop real-time monitoring systems for deployed
        ML models.

    –   Implement automated alerts for model
        performance degradation or data drift.

    –   Design and implement model retraining pipelines.

    –   Conduct regular model audits and health checks.

6. Data Pipeline Management

   – Design and maintain efficient data ingestion and
     preprocessing pipelines.

   – Implement data validation and quality checks.

   – Develop feature stores for ML applications.

   – Optimize data storage and retrieval for ML
     workloads.

7. ML Platform Development

   – Contribute to the development of internal ML
     platforms and tools.

   – Implement automated machine learning (AutoML)
     solutions.

   – Develop interfaces for non-technical users to
     interact with ML systems.

   – Create documentation and user guides for ML
     platforms.

8. Security and Compliance

   – Implement security best practices for ML systems
     (e.g., data encryption, access controls).

   – Ensure compliance with data protection
     regulations in ML pipelines.

   – Implement model governance and auditability
     features.

   – Collaborate with security teams to conduct regular
     security assessments of ML systems.

9. Collaboration and Knowledge Sharing

    –   Work closely with data scientists, software
        engineers, and product managers.

    –   Participate in code reviews and provide
        constructive feedback.

    –   Contribute to the development of best practices
        and coding standards for ML engineering.

    –   Mentor junior team members and conduct
        knowledge-sharing sessions.

10. Research and Innovation

    –   Stay up-to-date with the latest advancements in ML
        engineering and MLOps.

    –   Evaluate new tools and technologies for potential
        adoption.

    –   Contribute to open source ML projects and attend
        relevant conferences.

    –   Prototype innovative ML solutions to address
        business challenges.

Required Skills and Qualifications

1. Technical Skills

    –   Strong programming skills in Python, with
        experience in other languages like Java or Go

    –   Proficiency in ML frameworks such as TensorFlow,
        PyTorch, or scikit-learn

    –   Experience with cloud platforms (AWS, GCP, Azure)
        and their ML services

- Knowledge of containerization and orchestration technologies (Docker, Kubernetes)

- Familiarity with big data technologies (Spark, Hadoop)

- Understanding of RESTful APIs and microservices architecture

- Experience with version control systems (Git) and CI/CD tools (Jenkins, GitLab CI)

- Knowledge of SQL and NoSQL databases

2. Machine Learning Expertise

- Strong understanding of ML algorithms and their applications

- Experience with deep learning architectures and techniques

- Familiarity with ML model evaluation metrics and validation techniques

- Understanding of feature engineering and selection methods

3. MLOps and Software Engineering

- Experience with MLOps practices and tools (MLflow, Kubeflow, Airflow)

- Knowledge of software design patterns and best practices

- Familiarity with agile development methodologies

- Understanding of DevOps principles and practices

4. Data Management and Processing

   – Experience with data preprocessing and feature
     extraction techniques

   – Knowledge of data storage solutions and data lakes

   – Understanding of data privacy and security best
     practices

5. System Design and Architecture

   – Ability to design scalable and efficient ML systems

   – Experience with distributed systems and parallel
     computing

   – Knowledge of high-performance computing
     techniques

6. Soft Skills

   – Strong problem-solving and analytical skills

   – Excellent communication skills, both written
     and verbal

   – Ability to work effectively in cross-functional teams

   – Self-motivated with a passion for continuous learning

   – Attention to detail and commitment to code quality

7. Education and Experience

   – Bachelor's or master's degree in Computer Science,
     Engineering, or a related field

   – 3+ years of experience in software engineering or
     ML engineering roles

   – Proven track record of deploying ML models in
     production environments

8. Desirable Certifications

- Cloud certifications (AWS Certified Machine Learning, Google Cloud Professional Machine Learning Engineer)

- Kubernetes certifications (CKA, CKAD)

- Data Science or ML certifications (TensorFlow Developer Certificate, Azure AI Engineer)

The role of an ML engineer is becoming more critical with the increasing adoption of machine learning in production environments. The focus is shifting from traditional software engineering to MLOps, which involves managing the end-to-end machine learning lifecycle. This includes model operationalization, deployment, scaling, serving, and monitoring. The successful ML engineer of the future will need to have a deep understanding of machine learning models, software engineering, and system design.

Data Engineer

The key role of the data engineer is to design, implement, and maintain scalable data infrastructure that enables real-time data processing, efficient data storage, and seamless data access for analytics and machine learning applications. The role focuses on building robust data pipelines, managing data catalogs, and implementing feature stores to support advanced analytics and AI initiatives across the organization.

Key Responsibilities

1. Data Pipeline Development and Management

- Design and implement scalable, fault-tolerant data pipelines for batch and real-time processing.

- Develop ETL (Extract, Transform, Load) and ELT (Extract, Load, Transform) processes.

- Implement data quality checks and data validation processes within pipelines.

- Optimize data pipelines for performance and cost-efficiency.

- Implement data versioning and lineage tracking.

2. Real-time Data Processing Systems

- Design and implement streaming data architectures using technologies like Apache Kafka, Apache Flink, or Apache Spark Streaming.

- Develop real-time data ingestion and processing workflows.

- Implement event-driven architectures for real-time analytics.

- Ensure low-latency data delivery for time-sensitive applications.

3. Data Storage and Management

- Design and implement data storage solutions, including data lakes and data warehouses.

- Optimize data storage for performance, cost, and scalability.

- Implement data partitioning and indexing strategies.

- Manage data retention policies and archiving processes.

- Implement data encryption and access control mechanisms.

4. Data Catalog Management

– Implement and maintain a comprehensive data catalog system.

– Develop automated processes for metadata extraction and management.

– Ensure proper documentation of data assets, including their origin, transformations, and usage.

– Implement data discovery and search functionalities.

– Collaborate with data governance teams to maintain data lineage and compliance information.

5. Feature Store Development and Management

– Design and implement feature stores for machine learning applications.

– Develop processes for feature extraction, transformation, and storage.

– Implement feature versioning and tracking mechanisms.

– Ensure consistency between offline (batch) and online (real-time) feature serving.

– Optimize feature access for low-latency model inference.

6. Data Integration and APIs

– Develop and maintain APIs for data access and integration.

– Implement data synchronization between different systems and platforms.

– Ensure interoperability between various data sources and consumers.

– Implement caching mechanisms for frequently accessed data.

7. Cloud Data Infrastructure

– Design and implement cloud-based data architectures (e.g., using AWS, GCP, or Azure services).

– Optimize cloud resource utilization for cost-efficiency.

– Implement multi-region and multi-cloud data strategies.

– Ensure compliance with cloud security best practices.

8. Data Security and Compliance

– Implement data security measures, including encryption, access controls, and auditing.

– Ensure compliance with data protection regulations (e.g., GDPR, CCPA).

– Collaborate with security teams to conduct regular security assessments.

– Implement data masking and anonymization techniques for sensitive data.

9. Performance Monitoring and Optimization

– Implement monitoring and alerting systems for data infrastructure.

– Conduct performance tuning of databases and data processing systems.

    – Optimize query performance and develop query optimization strategies.

    – Implement auto-scaling solutions for handling variable workloads.

10. Collaboration and Knowledge Sharing

    – Work closely with data scientists, ML engineers, and analytics teams.

    – Provide guidance on best practices for data modeling and schema design.

    – Contribute to the development of data engineering standards and practices.

    – Mentor junior team members and conduct knowledge-sharing sessions.

11. Continuous Learning and Innovation

    – Stay up-to-date with the latest advancements in data engineering technologies.

    – Evaluate and recommend new tools and technologies for adoption.

    – Contribute to open source data engineering projects.

    – Participate in relevant conferences and community events.

Required Skills and Qualifications

1. Programming and Scripting

    – Proficiency in Python, Scala, or Java

    – Experience with SQL and NoSQL databases

    – Familiarity with shell scripting (Bash, PowerShell)

2. Data Processing Technologies

    – Expertise in big data technologies (Apache Hadoop ecosystem)

    – Experience with distributed computing frameworks (Apache Spark, Apache Flink)

    – Knowledge of stream processing systems (Apache Kafka, Apache Pulsar)

3. Data Storage and Databases

    – Experience with relational databases (PostgreSQL, MySQL)

    – Knowledge of NoSQL databases (MongoDB, Cassandra, HBase)

    – Familiarity with data warehousing solutions (Snowflake, Amazon Redshift, Google BigQuery)

    – Understanding of data lake architectures and technologies (Delta Lake, Apache Hudi)

4. Cloud Platforms and Services

    – Proficiency in at least one major cloud platform (AWS, GCP, Azure)

    – Experience with cloud-native data services (e.g., Amazon S3, Google Cloud Storage, Azure Data Lake)

    – Knowledge of server-less computing and containerization (Docker, Kubernetes)

5. Data Modeling and Design

    –   Strong understanding of data modeling techniques

    –   Experience with schema design for various data storage systems

    –   Knowledge of dimensional modeling and star schema design

6. ETL/ELT and Data Integration

    –   Experience with ETL/ELT tools and frameworks (Apache NiFi, Airflow, dbt)

    –   Knowledge of change data capture (CDC) techniques

    –   Understanding of data integration patterns and best practices

7. Data Governance and Metadata Management

    –   Familiarity with data governance frameworks and tools

    –   Experience with metadata management systems

    –   Understanding of data quality management processes

8. Performance Optimization

    –   Experience in database performance tuning

    –   Knowledge of query optimization techniques

    –   Understanding of distributed systems performance considerations

9. Security and Compliance

    –   Knowledge of data security best practices

    –   Understanding of data protection regulations

    –   Experience with data encryption and access control
        mechanisms

10. Soft Skills

    –   Strong problem-solving and analytical skills

    –   Excellent communication and collaboration
        abilities

    –   Ability to work in fast-paced, agile environments

    –   Attention to detail and commitment to data quality

11. Education and Experience

    –   Bachelor's or master's degree in Computer Science,
        Information Systems, or a related field

    –   3+ years of experience in data engineering roles

    –   Proven track record of building scalable data
        infrastructure

12. Desirable Certifications

    –   Cloud platform certifications (e.g., AWS Certified
        Data Analytics - Specialty, Google Cloud
        Professional Data Engineer)

    –   Apache Kafka certification

    –   Cloudera Certified Professional Data Engineer

The evolving role of a data engineer requires a combination of technical expertise in data processing technologies, cloud platforms, and data modeling, along with a strong understanding of modern data architectures and best practices. As organizations increasingly rely on real-time data and advanced analytics, data engineers play a crucial role in building and maintaining the data infrastructure that powers these initiatives.

Data Labeler/Data Analyst

The data labeler/analyst focuses on enhancing the quality and efficiency of machine learning models by providing high-quality labeled data, implementing active learning strategies, and maintaining feedback loops between model performance and data labeling processes. This role bridges the gap between raw data collection and model development, ensuring that AI systems are trained on accurate, relevant, and diverse datasets.

Key Responsibilities

1. Data Labeling and Annotation

   – Perform accurate and consistent labeling of various data types (text, images, audio, video).

   – Apply domain-specific knowledge to ensure high-quality annotations.

   – Use specialized annotation tools and platforms efficiently.

   – Adhere to labeling guidelines and maintain consistency across datasets.

   – Handle complex labeling tasks, including bounding boxes, segmentation, and entity recognition.

2. Quality Assurance and Control

    –   Conduct regular quality checks on labeled data.

    –   Implement and maintain labeling quality metrics.

    –   Identify and resolve inconsistencies or errors in labeled datasets.

    –   Participate in calibration exercises to ensure inter-annotator agreement.

3. Active Learning Implementation

    –   Collaborate with data scientists to implement active learning strategies.

    –   Identify and prioritize data samples for labeling based on model uncertainty.

    –   Provide feedback on the effectiveness of active learning approaches.

    –   Contribute to the development of custom active learning algorithms.

4. Feedback Loop Management

    –   Analyze model performance metrics to identify areas for improvement in labeled data.

    –   Implement processes for continuous refinement of labeled datasets based on model feedback.

    –   Collaborate with ML engineers to establish efficient feedback mechanisms between models and labeling processes.

    –   Contribute to the development of automated data correction and relabeling workflows.

5. Data Analysis and Insight Generation

   – Perform exploratory data analysis on raw and labeled datasets.

   – Identify patterns, trends, and anomalies in data that may impact labeling strategies.

   – Generate insights to improve labeling efficiency and accuracy.

   – Contribute to the development of data-driven labeling strategies.

6. Labeling Process Optimization

   – Analyze labeling workflows to identify bottlenecks and inefficiencies.

   – Propose and implement process improvements to enhance labeling speed and quality.

   – Evaluate and recommend new labeling tools and technologies.

   – Develop automation scripts to streamline repetitive labeling tasks.

7. Data Bias and Fairness Assessment

   – Identify potential biases in labeled datasets.

   – Implement strategies to ensure diverse and representative data samples.

   – Collaborate with ethics teams to address fairness concerns in data labeling.

   – Contribute to the development of bias mitigation strategies in data collection and labeling.

8. Documentation and Knowledge Management

   – Maintain comprehensive documentation of labeling processes and guidelines.

   – Develop and update training materials for new labelers.

   – Contribute to the creation of a knowledge base for common labeling challenges and solutions.

   – Participate in knowledge sharing sessions with the wider data team.

9. Collaboration with Cross-functional Teams

   – Work closely with data scientists and ML engineers to understand model requirements.

   – Collaborate with domain experts to ensure accurate interpretation of complex data.

   – Provide regular updates to project managers on labeling progress and challenges.

   – Participate in sprint planning and retrospectives to align labeling efforts with project goals.

10. Continuous Learning and Skill Development

   – Stay updated on the latest trends in data labeling, active learning, and ML model development.

   – Participate in relevant workshops, webinars, and training sessions.

   – Contribute to the data science community through blog posts or conference presentations.

   – Develop skills in emerging areas such as weak supervision and programmatic labeling.

Required Skills and Qualifications

1. Technical Skills

    – Proficiency in data annotation tools and platforms

    – Basic programming skills in Python or R for data analysis and automation

    – Familiarity with machine learning concepts and model evaluation metrics

    – Experience with data visualization tools (e.g., Matplotlib, Seaborn, Tableau)

    – Understanding of database systems and SQL for data querying

2. Data Analysis and Statistics

    – Strong analytical and problem-solving skills

    – Basic understanding of statistical concepts and data distributions

    – Experience with exploratory data analysis techniques

    – Ability to identify patterns and anomalies in large datasets

3. Domain Expertise

    – Specialized knowledge in relevant domains (e.g., computer vision, natural language processing, speech recognition)

    – Understanding of industry-specific terminology and concepts

    – Ability to apply domain knowledge to complex labeling tasks

4. Active Learning and ML Concepts

   – Familiarity with active learning principles and strategies

   – Basic understanding of machine learning workflows and model training processes

   – Knowledge of data preprocessing and feature engineering concepts

5. Quality Assurance and Attention to Detail

   – Strong focus on data quality and consistency

   – Experience with quality control processes and metrics

   – Ability to maintain high accuracy levels in repetitive tasks

6. Communication and Collaboration

   – Excellent written and verbal communication skills

   – Ability to work effectively in cross-functional teams

   – Experience in providing constructive feedback and suggestions for process improvement

7. Time Management and Productivity

   – Ability to manage multiple labeling projects simultaneously

   – Experience with project management tools and agile methodologies

   – Strong organizational skills and ability to meet deadlines

8. Ethical Considerations and Bias Awareness

   – Understanding of ethical implications in AI and data labeling

   – Awareness of potential biases in data and ability to implement mitigation strategies

   – Commitment to fairness and diversity in data representation

9. Adaptability and Continuous Learning

   – Willingness to learn new tools, technologies, and labeling techniques

   – Ability to adapt to changing project requirements and priorities

   – Interest in staying updated with the latest trends in data science and AI

10. Education and Experience

   – Bachelor's degree in Computer Science, Data Science, or a related field (or equivalent experience)

   – 2+ years of experience in data labeling, data analysis, or related roles

   – Demonstrated experience with active learning projects is a plus

11. Desirable Certifications

   – Certifications in specific data labeling platforms or tools

– Data analysis certifications (e.g., Google Data
  Analytics Professional Certificate)

– Domain-specific certifications relevant to the
  industry (e.g., healthcare, finance)

The evolving role of a data labeler and analyst requires a unique combination of attention to detail, analytical skills, and understanding of machine learning processes. As AI systems become more sophisticated, the importance of high-quality, diverse, and well-curated training data increases, making this role crucial in the development of effective and unbiased AI models.

Model Governance Manager/Director

Model governance ensures the responsible development, deployment, and use of AI and machine learning models across the organization, with a focus on explainability, interpretability, fairness, and ethical considerations.

Key Responsibilities

1. Explainability and Interpretability Oversight

   – Develop and implement frameworks for assessing
     model explainability and interpretability.

   – Collaborate with data scientists and ML engineers
     to integrate explainable AI (XAI) techniques into
     model development processes.

   – Evaluate and approve explainability methods for
     different model types and use cases.

   – Ensure that model outputs can be interpreted and
     explained to stakeholders, including regulators and
     end users.

2. Fairness and Bias Mitigation

    –   Establish guidelines and metrics for assessing
        model fairness across different
        demographic groups.

    –   Implement processes to detect and mitigate bias in
        training data and model outputs.

    –   Collaborate with legal and compliance teams to
        ensure models meet regulatory requirements for
        non-discrimination.

    –   Develop and maintain a fairness monitoring system
        for deployed models.

3. Ethical AI Framework Development

    –   Create and maintain an ethical AI framework
        aligned with organizational values and industry
        best practices.

    –   Conduct ethical impact assessments for high-risk
        AI applications.

    –   Facilitate discussions and decision-making on
        ethical dilemmas related to AI deployment.

4. Model Risk Assessment and Validation

    –   Oversee the model validation process, integrating
        new considerations for explainability and fairness.

    –   Develop risk assessment methodologies that
        account for the unique challenges of advanced
        AI models.

    –   Implement continuous monitoring systems to
        detect model drift and performance degradation.

5. Regulatory Compliance and Reporting

    –   Stay informed about evolving AI regulations and
        ensure organizational compliance.

    –   Prepare documentation and reports for regulatory
        submissions related to AI models.

    –   Act as a liaison between the organization and
        regulatory bodies on matters of AI governance.

6. Stakeholder Education and Communication

    –   Develop training programs to educate stakeholders
        on model governance principles, explainability,
        and fairness.

    –   Communicate model governance policies and
        decisions to executive leadership.

    –   Facilitate cross-functional collaboration between
        data science, legal, compliance, and
        business teams.

7. Governance Policy Development and
    Implementation

    –   Create and maintain model governance policies
        that reflect the latest in AI ethics and best practices.

    –   Establish approval processes for the development
        and deployment of high-risk AI models.

    –   Implement governance tools and platforms to
        streamline the model lifecycle management
        process.

8. Incident Response and Model Decommissioning

   – Develop protocols for responding to model failures or ethical breaches.

   – Oversee the process of model decommissioning when necessary, ensuring proper data handling and system updates.

9. Research and Innovation

   – Stay abreast of emerging techniques in explainable AI, fairness in machine learning, and ethical AI.

   – Collaborate with academic institutions and industry partners on research initiatives.

   – Contribute to the development of industry standards for AI governance.

10. Performance Metrics and Reporting

   – Develop KPIs for measuring the effectiveness of the model governance program.

   – Prepare regular reports on model governance activities, risks, and opportunities for improvement.

   – Present findings and recommendations to executive leadership and board committees.

Required Skills and Qualifications

1. Advanced degree in computer science, statistics, or a related field

2. Strong understanding of machine learning algorithms and AI technologies

3. Experience in risk management, compliance, or auditing in a technology-focused environment

4. Knowledge of relevant regulations and ethical frameworks related to AI

5. Excellent communication and interpersonal skills

6. Ability to bridge technical and non-technical stakeholders

7. Strong analytical and problem-solving skills

8. Demonstrated leadership and project management experience

The model governance manager/director plays a crucial role in ensuring that AI models are not only accurate and efficient but also transparent, fair, and ethically sound. This position requires a unique blend of technical expertise, ethical considerations, and strategic thinking to navigate the complex landscape of advanced AI deployment in organizational settings.

Data Governance Manager/Director

The primary objective of data governance professionals is to oversee the organization's data governance strategy, ensuring data quality, privacy, and compliance throughout the data lifecycle, with a particular focus on managing synthetic data and adapting to evolving data privacy requirements in the age of AI and advanced analytics.

Key Responsibilities

1. Data Lifecycle Management

   – Develop and implement comprehensive data lifecycle management strategies.

   – Oversee data creation, storage, usage, archiving, and deletion processes.

- Implement data classification schemes to ensure appropriate handling of different data types.

- Establish protocols for data retention and disposal, considering legal and business requirements.

2. Synthetic Data Management

- Develop policies and procedures for the creation, use, and management of synthetic data.

- Collaborate with data science teams to ensure synthetic data meets quality and privacy standards.

- Oversee the integration of synthetic data into existing data ecosystems.

- Establish guidelines for validating synthetic data and assessing its fitness for various use cases.

3. Data Privacy and Protection

- Develop and maintain data privacy policies aligned with global regulations (e.g., GDPR, CCPA).

- Implement privacy-by-design principles in data management processes.

- Oversee data anonymization and pseudonymization techniques.

- Conduct regular privacy impact assessments and data protection audits.

- Collaborate with legal and compliance teams to ensure adherence to data privacy laws.

4. Data Quality Management

   – Establish data quality standards and metrics across the organization.

   – Implement data quality monitoring and improvement processes.

   – Oversee data cleansing and enrichment initiatives.

   – Develop strategies for maintaining data accuracy, completeness, and consistency.

5. Data Access and Security

   – Define and enforce data access policies and controls.

   – Implement role-based access control (RBAC) for data resources.

   – Oversee data encryption and security measures for data at rest and in transit.

   – Collaborate with IT security teams to ensure robust data protection measures.

6. Metadata Management

   – Develop and maintain a comprehensive metadata repository.

   – Implement data cataloging and data lineage tracking systems.

   – Ensure proper documentation of data sources, transformations, and usage.

7. Data Ethics and Responsible AI

   – Develop ethical guidelines for data usage,
     particularly in AI and advanced analytics.

   – Oversee the ethical implications of data collection,
     processing, and analysis.

   – Collaborate with AI ethics committees to ensure
     responsible use of data in AI systems.

8. Compliance and Regulatory Management

   – Stay informed about evolving data regulations and
     ensure organizational compliance.

   – Prepare documentation and reports for regulatory
     submissions related to data management.

   – Act as a liaison between the organization and
     regulatory bodies on data governance matters.

9. Data Governance Tools and Technologies

   – Evaluate and implement data governance tools and
     platforms.

   – Oversee the integration of data governance
     technologies with existing IT infrastructure.

   – Ensure the adoption of data governance tools
     across the organization.

10. Stakeholder Education and Communication

   – Develop training programs on data governance
     principles, privacy, and best practices.

   – Promote a data-driven culture within the
     organization.

- Communicate data governance policies and decisions to executive leadership.

- Facilitate cross-functional collaboration between IT, legal, compliance, and business teams.

11. Data Incident Response

- Develop and maintain data breach response plans.

- Coordinate with IT security and legal teams in the event of a data incident.

- Oversee the post-incident analysis and implementation of preventive measures.

12. Performance Metrics and Reporting

- Develop KPIs for measuring the effectiveness of the data governance program.

- Prepare regular reports on data governance activities, risks, and opportunities for improvement.

- Present findings and recommendations to executive leadership and board committees.

13. Innovation and Research

- Stay abreast of emerging trends in data governance, privacy-enhancing technologies, and synthetic data generation.

- Collaborate with academic institutions and industry partners on research initiatives.

- Contribute to the development of industry standards for data governance.

Required Skills and Qualifications

1. Advanced degree in information management, computer science, or a related field

2. Strong understanding of data management principles, privacy regulations, and emerging technologies

3. Experience in data governance, compliance, or risk management in a technology-focused environment

4. Knowledge of data protection laws and regulations (e.g., GDPR, CCPA)

5. Familiarity with data governance tools and technologies

6. Excellent communication and interpersonal skills

7. Ability to translate complex technical concepts for non-technical stakeholders

8. Strong analytical and problem-solving skills

9. Demonstrated leadership and project management experience

10. Certification in data governance or privacy (e.g., CDMP, CIPP) is a plus

The data governance manager/director plays a crucial role in ensuring that an organization's data assets are managed effectively, securely, and ethically in the face of rapidly evolving technologies and regulatory landscapes. This position requires a unique blend of technical knowledge, strategic thinking, and leadership skills to navigate the complex intersection of data management, privacy, and innovation.

DevOps Manager/Director

The key roles of the DevOps manager/director for ML and Gen AI are to lead and oversee the development, deployment, and operation of machine learning (ML) and generative AI (Gen AI) systems at scale, ensuring seamless integration of ML models into production environments, maintaining high performance, reliability, and security while fostering a culture of continuous improvement and innovation.

Key Responsibilities

1. MLOps Strategy and Implementation

    – Develop and execute MLOps strategies aligned with organizational goals.

    – Design and implement end-to-end ML/AI pipelines for model development, testing, deployment, and monitoring.

    – Establish best practices for version control, continuous integration, and continuous deployment (CI/CD) for ML models.

    – Implement infrastructure-as-code practices for ML environments.

2. ML Infrastructure Management

    – Design and maintain scalable infrastructure for ML model training, testing, and deployment.

    – Implement and manage cloud-based ML platforms (e.g., AWS SageMaker, Google AI Platform, Azure ML).

    – Optimize resource allocation and cost management for ML workloads.

    – Ensure high availability and fault tolerance of ML systems.

3. Automated ML Pipeline Development

    –   Oversee the development of automated pipelines for data preparation, feature engineering, and model training.

    –   Implement automated testing frameworks for ML models, including unit tests, integration tests, and A/B tests.

    –   Develop strategies for model versioning and experiment tracking.

4. Model Deployment and Serving

    –   Design and implement efficient model serving architectures for both batch and real-time inference.

    –   Optimize model deployment processes for minimal downtime and seamless updates.

    –   Implement canary deployments and rollback strategies for ML models.

    –   Ensure scalability and performance of deployed models under varying loads.

5. Monitoring and Observability

    –   Implement comprehensive monitoring systems for ML model performance, data drift, and system health.

    –   Develop dashboards and alerting systems for real-time visibility into ML operations.

    –   Establish key performance indicators (KPIs) for ML systems and track them consistently.

    –   Implement logging and tracing solutions for ML pipelines and model inferences.

6. Security and Compliance

   – Ensure ML systems adhere to security best
     practices and compliance requirements.

   – Implement access controls, encryption, and secure
     communication for ML pipelines and data.

   – Collaborate with security teams to conduct regular
     security assessments of ML infrastructure.

   – Stay updated on regulations affecting AI/ML
     deployments and ensure compliance.

7. Gen AI Model Lifecycle Management

   – Develop strategies for managing the lifecycle of
     large language models and other generative
     AI models.

   – Implement efficient fine-tuning and adaptation
     processes for pre-trained models.

   – Design systems for continuous learning and model
     updates in production.

   – Manage the complexities of deploying and serving
     large-scale generative models.

8. Performance Optimization

   – Continuously optimize ML pipelines and
     infrastructure for improved efficiency and
     reduced costs.

   – Implement strategies for distributed training and
     inference.

- Optimize model serving for low-latency and high-throughput scenarios.

- Conduct regular performance audits and implement improvements.

9. Collaboration and Knowledge Sharing

- Foster collaboration between data scientists, ML engineers, and software developers.

- Establish communication channels between ML teams and other IT operations teams.

- Develop and maintain documentation for MLOps processes and best practices.

- Conduct training sessions and workshops on MLOps tools and methodologies.

10. Innovation and Research

- Stay abreast of the latest advancements in MLOps, DevOps for AI, and Gen AI technologies.

- Evaluate and recommend new tools and technologies for adoption.

- Encourage experimentation and innovation in ML infrastructure and deployment strategies.

- Collaborate with academic and industry partners on cutting-edge MLOps research.

11. Team Leadership and Development

- Build and lead high-performing MLOps teams.

- Mentor team members and foster their professional growth.

- Establish clear goals and KPIs for the MLOps function.

- Promote a culture of continuous learning and improvement.

Required Skills and Qualifications

1. Technical Expertise

   - Strong background in software engineering and DevOps practices

   - Solid understanding of machine learning algorithms and workflows

   - Proficiency in programming languages such as Python, Go, or Java

   - Experience with containerization technologies (Docker, Kubernetes)

   - Familiarity with ML frameworks (TensorFlow, PyTorch) and MLOps tools (MLflow, Kubeflow)

2. Cloud and Infrastructure

   - Extensive experience with cloud platforms (AWS, GCP, Azure) and their ML services

   - Knowledge of infrastructure-as-code tools (Terraform, CloudFormation)

   - Experience with distributed systems and microservices architectures

   - Understanding of networking concepts and security best practices

3. CI/CD and Automation

   – Expertise in CI/CD tools and practices (Jenkins, GitLab CI, GitHub Actions)

   – Experience in automating ML workflows and pipelines

   – Knowledge of configuration management tools (Ansible, Puppet)

4. Data Management and Processing

   – Understanding of data processing at scale (Spark, Hadoop)

   – Experience with data versioning and feature stores

   – Familiarity with data governance and compliance requirements

5. Monitoring and Observability

   – Experience with monitoring tools (Prometheus, Grafana, ELK stack)

   – Knowledge of log management and analysis

   – Understanding of ML-specific monitoring requirements (model drift, data quality)

6. Security and Compliance

   – Strong knowledge of security best practices for ML systems

   – Understanding of relevant regulations (GDPR, CCPA) and their impact on ML deployments

   – Experience in implementing secure ML pipelines

7. Gen AI and Large Language Models

   – Understanding of the unique challenges in deploying and managing large language models

   – Familiarity with techniques for efficient serving of generative models

   – Knowledge of ethical considerations in deploying Gen AI systems

8. Leadership and Management

   – Proven experience in leading technical teams

   – Strong project management and organizational skills

   – Ability to communicate complex technical concepts to both technical and non-technical stakeholders

   – Experience in budget management and resource allocation

9. Problem-Solving and Innovation

   – Strong analytical and problem-solving skills

   – Ability to innovate and find creative solutions to complex MLOps challenges

   – Forward-thinking approach to anticipate future ML infrastructure needs

10. Soft Skills

   – Excellent communication and interpersonal skills

   – Ability to work effectively in cross-functional teams

- Adaptability and willingness to learn in a rapidly evolving field

- Strong ethical judgment and commitment to responsible AI practices

11. Education and Experience

- Bachelor's or master's degree in Computer Science, Engineering, or a related field

- 8+ years of experience in DevOps, software engineering, or related roles

- 3+ years of experience specifically in ML/AI operations or similar roles

- Proven track record of successfully implementing MLOps practices at scale

12. Desirable Certifications

- Cloud platform certifications (AWS Certified DevOps Engineer, Google Cloud Professional DevOps Engineer)

- Kubernetes certifications (CKA, CKAD)

- MLOps certifications (e.g., MLOps Engineering on GCP)

The role of a DevOps manager/director for ML and Gen AI is crucial in bridging the gap between traditional software development practices and the unique challenges posed by machine learning and generative AI systems. This position requires a blend of technical expertise, leadership skills, and strategic thinking to effectively manage the entire lifecycle of ML/AI systems from development to production, ensuring scalability, reliability, and innovation in AI-driven organizations.

Model Risk Manager/Auditor

The primary objective of this role is to ensure the integrity, fairness, and compliance of machine learning (ML) and generative AI (Gen AI) models used in critical decision-making processes across the organization. This role focuses on developing and implementing comprehensive risk management frameworks, conducting thorough model audits, and ensuring adherence to regulatory requirements and ethical AI principles.

Key Responsibilities

1. Model Risk Framework Development

    –   Design and implement a robust model risk management framework specific to ML and Gen AI models.

    –   Establish policies, procedures, and guidelines for model development, validation, and deployment.

    –   Define risk appetite and tolerance levels for various types of ML/AI models.

    –   Develop model inventories and risk classification systems.

2. Model Validation and Testing

    –   Conduct independent validation of ML and Gen AI models.

    –   Design and implement rigorous testing procedures for model accuracy, stability, and robustness.

    –   Assess model performance across different scenarios and stress conditions.

    –   Validate the appropriateness of data sources, feature engineering processes, and model architectures.

3. Bias and Fairness Assessment

    –   Develop and implement methodologies to detect
        and mitigate bias in ML/AI models.

    –   Conduct fairness assessments across different
        demographic groups.

    –   Implement tools and techniques for measuring and
        monitoring algorithmic fairness.

    –   Collaborate with legal and compliance teams to
        ensure adherence to anti-discrimination laws.

4. Explainability and Interpretability

    –   Assess the explainability of complex ML and Gen
        AI models.

    –   Implement and evaluate various explainable AI
        (XAI) techniques.

    –   Ensure that model decisions can be interpreted and
        explained to stakeholders and regulators.

    –   Develop guidelines for appropriate use of black-box
        vs. interpretable models.

5. Regulatory Compliance

    –   Stay abreast of evolving regulations and guidelines
        related to AI/ML in various jurisdictions.

    –   Ensure compliance with relevant regulations (e.g.,
        GDPR, FCRA, CCPA).

    –   Prepare documentation and reports for regulatory
        submissions and audits.

    –   Collaborate with legal teams to interpret and
        implement regulatory requirements.

6. Model Governance and Documentation

   – Establish and maintain comprehensive model documentation standards.

   – Oversee the development of model cards, datasheets, and other governance artifacts.

   – Implement version control and change management processes for models and associated documentation.

   – Ensure traceability of model decisions and changes over time.

7. Ethical AI Oversight

   – Develop and implement ethical AI guidelines and principles.

   – Conduct ethical impact assessments for high-risk AI applications.

   – Collaborate with ethics committees and boards on AI-related decisions.

   – Foster a culture of responsible AI development and use across the organization.

8. Risk Monitoring and Reporting

   – Implement ongoing monitoring processes for deployed ML and Gen AI models.

   – Develop key risk indicators (KRIs) and monitoring dashboards.

   – Prepare regular risk reports for senior management and board committees.

   – Establish escalation procedures for identified model risks.

9. Incident Response and Model Decommissioning

    –   Develop and implement incident response plans
        for model failures or ethical breaches.

    –   Oversee the process of model decommissioning
        and replacement.

    –   Conduct post-incident analyses and implement
        lessons learned.

10. Stakeholder Education and Communication

    –   Educate senior management and board members
        on ML/AI model risks.

    –   Conduct training sessions on model risk
        management for relevant staff.

    –   Communicate model risk assessments and
        recommendations to various stakeholders.

    –   Act as a liaison between technical teams, business
        units, and regulators on model risk matters.

11. Collaboration with Model Development Teams

    –   Work closely with data scientists and ML engineers
        to integrate risk considerations into the model
        development lifecycle.

    –   Provide guidance on risk mitigation strategies
        during model design and implementation.

    –   Facilitate a culture of risk awareness in AI/
        ML teams.

12. Continuous Improvement and Research

   – Stay updated on emerging model risk management techniques and best practices.

   – Conduct research on novel approaches to managing risks in advanced AI systems.

   – Contribute to industry standards and guidelines for AI/ML model risk management.

   – Participate in relevant conferences and forums to share knowledge and learn from peers.

Required Skills and Qualifications

1. Technical Knowledge

   – Strong understanding of machine learning algorithms and architectures

   – Familiarity with deep learning and generative AI technologies

   – Proficiency in programming languages used in data science (e.g., Python, R)

   – Understanding of data processing and feature engineering techniques

2. Risk Management Expertise

   – In-depth knowledge of risk management principles and frameworks

   – Experience in financial or operational risk management

   – Understanding of model risk concepts and best practices

3. Statistical and Mathematical Skills

   – Strong foundation in statistics and probability theory

   – Knowledge of statistical testing and hypothesis evaluation

   – Familiarity with quantitative risk assessment techniques

4. Regulatory and Compliance Knowledge

   – Thorough understanding of relevant regulations affecting AI/ML models

   – Experience in interpreting and implementing regulatory guidelines

   – Knowledge of industry standards and best practices in model governance

5. Ethical AI and Fairness

   – Understanding of ethical AI principles and frameworks

   – Knowledge of fairness metrics and bias mitigation techniques

   – Familiarity with the societal impacts of AI systems

6. Auditing and Validation Skills

   – Experience in conducting model audits or validations

   – Ability to design and implement testing procedures for complex systems

   – Critical thinking and attention to detail

7. Communication and Interpersonal Skills

   – Excellent written and verbal communication skills

   – Ability to explain complex technical concepts to non-technical stakeholders

   – Strong presentation and reporting skills

8. Analytical and Problem-Solving Abilities

   – Strong analytical skills and logical reasoning

   – Ability to identify and assess complex risks in AI systems

   – Creative problem-solving skills for novel AI risk scenarios

9. Leadership and Influence

   – Ability to influence decision-makers and drive change

   – Experience in leading cross-functional teams or projects

   – Skills in building consensus among diverse stakeholders

10. Industry and Domain Knowledge

   – Understanding of the specific industry where AI/ ML models are applied

   – Familiarity with domain-specific regulations and risk considerations

11. Continuous Learning Mindset

   – Commitment to staying updated on rapid advancements in AI/ML technologies

   – Willingness to adapt risk management practices to emerging AI paradigms

12. Education and Experience

   – Master's degree or higher in a relevant field (e.g., Computer Science, Statistics, Mathematics, Risk Management)

   – 5+ years of experience in model risk management, preferably with focus on ML/AI

   – Professional certifications in risk management (e.g., FRM, PRM) or AI ethics are a plus

13. Desirable Certifications

   – Certified in Risk and Information Systems Control (CRISC)

   – Certified Information Systems Auditor (CISA)

   – Professional certifications in AI ethics or responsible AI

The role of a model risk manager/auditor for ML and Gen AI is crucial in ensuring that advanced AI systems are deployed responsibly, ethically, and in compliance with regulatory requirements. This position requires a unique blend of technical knowledge, risk management expertise, and strategic thinking to effectively navigate the complex landscape of AI governance and risk mitigation.

Machine Learning Architect

This key role is to design, develop, and oversee the implementation of advanced machine learning and generative AI systems that align with organizational goals and industry best practices. The ML architect is responsible for creating scalable, efficient, and innovative AI solutions while ensuring their integration with existing systems and processes.

Key Responsibilities

1. AI Strategy and Architecture Design

    – Develop the overall AI strategy and roadmap for the organization.

    – Design scalable and robust architectures for ML and Gen AI systems.

    – Create blueprints for end-to-end ML pipelines, from data ingestion to model deployment.

    – Ensure alignment of AI initiatives with business objectives and technical capabilities.

2. Model Development and Optimization

    – Lead the design and development of complex ML and Gen AI models.

    – Implement advanced techniques such as transfer learning, multi-task learning, and meta-learning.

    – Optimize model architectures for performance, efficiency, and scalability.

    – Develop custom loss functions and training regimes for specific use cases.

3. Infrastructure Planning and Management

   – Design and oversee the implementation of infrastructure for ML model training and deployment.

   – Optimize resource allocation for high-performance computing in AI workloads.

   – Implement strategies for distributed and parallel computing in ML systems.

   – Collaborate with DevOps teams to ensure seamless integration of ML systems with existing infrastructure.

4. Data Architecture and Engineering

   – Design data architectures that support large-scale ML and Gen AI systems.

   – Develop strategies for efficient data ingestion, processing, and feature engineering.

   – Implement data versioning and feature store solutions.

   – Ensure data quality, consistency, and availability for ML pipelines.

5. MLOps and Automation

   – Design and implement MLOps practices for continuous integration and deployment of ML models.

   – Develop automated workflows for model training, evaluation, and deployment.

   – Implement model versioning, experiment tracking, and reproducibility solutions.

- Collaborate with DevOps teams to integrate ML workflows into existing CI/CD pipelines.

6. Performance Monitoring and Optimization

   - Design systems for continuous monitoring of ML model performance in production.

   - Implement techniques for detecting and addressing model drift and data shift.

   - Develop strategies for model updates and retraining in production environments.

   - Optimize inference speed and resource utilization for deployed models.

7. Research and Innovation

   - Stay abreast of the latest advancements in ML and Gen AI technologies.

   - Conduct research on novel ML architectures and techniques.

   - Lead proof-of-concept projects to evaluate new AI technologies.

   - Contribute to the AI community through publications, open source projects, or conference presentations.

8. Cross-functional Collaboration

   - Work closely with data scientists, software engineers, and product managers.

   - Collaborate with domain experts to incorporate subject matter expertise into AI solutions.

- Provide guidance and mentorship to junior ML engineers and data scientists.

- Communicate complex AI concepts to non-technical stakeholders.

9. Ethical AI and Governance

- Ensure AI systems adhere to ethical AI principles and guidelines.

- Implement strategies for model interpretability and explainability.

- Collaborate with legal and compliance teams to address regulatory requirements.

- Develop frameworks for assessing and mitigating AI bias and fairness issues.

10. Security and Privacy

- Design AI systems with built-in security and privacy measures.

- Implement techniques for privacy-preserving machine learning (e.g., federated learning, differential privacy).

- Ensure compliance with data protection regulations in AI systems.

- Collaborate with security teams to address AI-specific security challenges.

11. Vendor and Technology Evaluation

- Evaluate and recommend AI platforms, tools, and services.

- Assess the feasibility and impact of integrating third-party AI solutions.

- Develop strategies for leveraging cloud-based AI services effectively.

- Manage relationships with AI technology vendors and service providers.

Required Skills and Qualifications

1. Technical Expertise

   - Deep understanding of ML algorithms, deep learning architectures, and Gen AI models

   - Proficiency in programming languages such as Python, Java, or C++

   - Expertise in ML frameworks (TensorFlow, PyTorch) and libraries (scikit-learn, Hugging Face)

   - Strong knowledge of distributed computing and big data technologies (Spark, Hadoop)

2. System Design and Architecture

   - Extensive experience in designing large-scale, distributed systems

   - Knowledge of microservices architecture and API design

   - Understanding of cloud computing platforms (AWS, GCP, Azure) and their ML services

   - Experience with containerization and orchestration (Docker, Kubernetes)

3. Data Engineering and Analytics

   – Strong understanding of data modeling, ETL processes, and data warehousing

   – Experience with SQL and NoSQL databases

   – Knowledge of data streaming technologies (Kafka, Flink)

   – Familiarity with data visualization tools and techniques

4. MLOps and DevOps

   – Experience with MLOps tools and practices (MLflow, Kubeflow, DVC)

   – Understanding of CI/CD pipelines and automation tools

   – Knowledge of monitoring and logging systems for ML (Prometheus, ELK stack)

5. Research and Innovation Skills

   – Strong background in AI research, preferably with publications or patents

   – Ability to quickly understand and implement new ML techniques

   – Experience in conducting and overseeing AI research projects

6. Problem-Solving and Analytical Skills

   – Exceptional problem-solving abilities for complex AI challenges

   – Strong analytical skills and attention to detail

- Ability to break down complex problems into manageable components

7. Leadership and Communication

   - Experience in leading technical teams and mentoring junior staff

   - Excellent verbal and written communication skills

   - Ability to translate complex technical concepts for non-technical audiences

   - Strong project management and organizational skills

8. Ethical AI and Governance

   - Understanding of ethical AI principles and their practical implementation

   - Familiarity with AI governance frameworks and best practices

   - Knowledge of relevant AI regulations and compliance requirements

9. Business Acumen

   - Ability to align AI solutions with business objectives and ROI

   - Understanding of industry-specific AI applications and use cases

   - Experience in translating business requirements into technical specifications

10. Continuous Learning

    – Commitment to staying updated with the rapidly
      evolving AI landscape

    – Active participation in AI communities and
      professional networks

    – Willingness to experiment with and evaluate
      emerging AI technologies

11. Education and Experience

    – PhD or master's degree in Computer Science, AI,
      Machine Learning, or a related field

    – 8+ years of experience in designing and
      implementing ML systems at scale

    – Proven track record of successful AI project
      deliveries in complex environments

12. Desirable Certifications

    – Cloud platform ML certifications (e.g., AWS
      Machine Learning Specialty, Google Professional
      Machine Learning Engineer)

    – Advanced AI/ML certifications from recognized
      institutions

    – Relevant open source project contributions or
      maintainer status

The role of a machine learning architect is crucial in guiding
organizations through the complexities of advanced AI systems. This
position requires a unique blend of deep technical expertise, strategic
thinking, and leadership skills to effectively design and implement cutting-
edge AI solutions that drive business value while addressing critical
aspects such as scalability, ethics, and governance.

Citizen Data Scientist

A citizen data scientist is an emerging role that bridges the gap between traditional business roles and specialized data science positions. Their primary responsibility is to democratize data analysis and AI technologies within an organization. Here's an overview of their key responsibilities and required skills.

Job Responsibilities

1. Data Analysis: Conduct basic to intermediate level data analysis using various tools and platforms.

2. AI/ML Model Usage: Utilize pre-built machine learning models and AI tools to derive insights and solve business problems.

3. Data Visualization: Create clear, impactful visualizations to communicate findings to non-technical stakeholders.

4. Process Optimization: Identify areas where data science and AI can improve business processes.

5. Cross-functional Collaboration: Work with different departments to understand their data needs and potential AI applications.

6. Knowledge Sharing: Educate colleagues on the benefits and basic concepts of data science and AI.

7. Generative AI Adoption: Promote and facilitate the use of generative AI tools within the organization.

8. Ethical Considerations: Ensure responsible use of data and AI technologies, considering privacy and ethical implications.

Required Skills and Qualifications

1. Basic Data Literacy: Understanding of data types, structures, and basic statistical concepts

2. Tool Proficiency: Familiarity with user-friendly data analysis and visualization tools (e.g., Tableau, Power BI, Excel)

3. Programming Basics: Elementary knowledge of programming languages like Python or R

4. AI/ML Fundamentals: Understanding of basic machine learning concepts and generative AI capabilities

5. Business Acumen: Strong understanding of business processes and ability to translate data insights into business value

6. Problem-Solving: Ability to approach business challenges with a data-driven mindset

7. Communication: Excellent skills in explaining complex concepts to non-technical audiences

8. Continuous Learning: Willingness to stay updated on emerging data science and AI trends

9. Critical Thinking: Ability to interpret data results and understand their limitations

10. Collaboration: Strong teamwork skills and ability to work across different departments

This role aims to make data science and AI more accessible within organizations, enabling a wider range of employees to leverage these technologies for business improvement. The exact responsibilities and skill requirements may vary depending on the organization's specific needs and level of data maturity.

ML Product Manager

An ML product manager plays a crucial role in guiding the development and implementation of machine learning and AI-driven products. As ML and generative AI become increasingly complex and integrated into critical business applications, the responsibilities and required skills for this role have evolved. Here's an overview.

Job Responsibilities

1. Product Strategy: Develop and maintain the product roadmap for ML/AI-driven applications, aligning with business goals and market needs.

2. Requirements Gathering: Work with stakeholders to identify and prioritize ML use cases and translate business needs into technical requirements.

3. Cross-functional Leadership: Coordinate between data scientists, engineers, UX designers, and business teams to ensure successful product development and deployment.

4. Model Lifecycle Management: Oversee the entire lifecycle of ML models, from conception to deployment and ongoing maintenance.

5. Performance Monitoring: Establish KPIs for ML models and products, and continuously monitor their performance and impact on business outcomes.

6. Ethical Oversight: Ensure responsible AI practices, addressing issues like bias, fairness, transparency, and privacy.

7. Risk Management: Identify and mitigate risks associated with ML model failures or unexpected behaviors, especially in mission-critical applications.

8. Vendor Management: Evaluate and manage relationships with ML/AI tool vendors and service providers.

9. User Adoption: Develop strategies to drive user adoption of ML-powered features and products.

10. Compliance: Ensure ML products adhere to relevant regulations and industry standards.

11. Innovation: Stay informed about the latest ML/AI technologies and identify opportunities for their application in products.

Required Skills and Qualifications

1. Technical Understanding: Strong grasp of ML/AI concepts, common algorithms, and their applications. Familiarity with generative AI technologies

2. Data Literacy: Ability to understand and work with complex datasets, and knowledge of data processing pipelines

3. Product Management Fundamentals: Proficiency in core product management skills like user story creation, prioritization, and agile methodologies

4. Business Acumen: Understanding of how ML/AI can drive business value and impact various industries

5. Strategic Thinking: Ability to develop long-term visions for AI-driven products and navigate the rapidly evolving AI landscape

6. Communication: Excellent skills in explaining complex ML concepts to both technical and non-technical audiences

7. Ethical Awareness: Understanding of AI ethics and ability to navigate the ethical implications of AI deployment

8. Technical Project Management: Experience managing complex technical projects, ideally involving data science or ML components

9. UX/UI Knowledge: Understanding of how to design intuitive user experiences for ML-powered products

10. Analytical Skills: Ability to interpret model performance metrics and translate them into product decisions

11. Stakeholder Management: Strong skills in managing expectations and aligning diverse stakeholders around a common vision

12. Continuous Learning: Commitment to staying updated on the latest ML/AI advancements and industry trends

13. Problem-Solving: Ability to tackle complex, ambiguous problems often encountered in ML product development

14. Risk Assessment: Capability to evaluate and mitigate risks associated with ML model deployment in critical applications

This role requires a unique blend of technical knowledge, product management skills, and strategic thinking. The ML product manager must navigate the complexities of cutting-edge technology while ensuring that the resulting products deliver tangible business value and meet user needs.

ML SecOps Manager/Director

An ML SecOps (Machine Learning Security Operations) manager/director is a critical role that has emerged to address the unique security challenges posed by ML and AI systems in enterprise environments. This position is responsible for safeguarding ML/AI assets and managing the associated risks. Here's an overview of the job responsibilities and required skills.

Job Responsibilities

1. Security Strategy: Develop and implement a comprehensive security strategy for ML/AI systems, aligning with overall enterprise security policies.

2. Risk Assessment: Conduct regular risk assessments of ML/AI systems, identifying vulnerabilities in data, models, and deployment pipelines.

3. Compliance Management: Ensure ML/AI systems comply with relevant regulations (e.g., GDPR, CCPA) and industry standards.

4. Incident Response: Develop and maintain incident response plans specific to ML/AI security breaches or failures.

5. Model Security: Implement measures to protect ML models from attacks such as model inversion, model stealing, or adversarial attacks.

6. Data Protection: Oversee the security of training data, including data anonymization, encryption, and access control.

7. Supply Chain Security: Manage security risks associated with third-party ML/AI tools, frameworks, and pre-trained models.

8. Monitoring and Auditing: Implement continuous monitoring systems for ML/AI operations and conduct regular security audits.

9. Security Training: Develop and deliver ML/AI security training programs for data scientists, engineers, and other relevant staff.

10. Ethical AI Oversight: Ensure ML/AI systems adhere to ethical AI principles, managing risks related to bias, fairness, and transparency.

11. Governance: Establish governance frameworks for secure ML/AI development, deployment, and operation.

12. Collaboration: Work closely with other departments (Legal, Compliance, Risk Management, Data Science) to address ML/AI security holistically.

13. Crisis Management: Lead the response to any security incidents or breaches related to ML/AI systems, minimizing financial and reputational damage.

14. Vendor Management: Evaluate and manage relationships with ML/AI security tool vendors and service providers.

Required Skills and Qualifications

1. Cybersecurity Expertise: Strong background in information security, with specific knowledge of ML/AI security challenges

2. ML/AI Knowledge: Solid understanding of machine learning and AI concepts, architectures, and development processes

3. Risk Management: Proficiency in enterprise risk management frameworks and their application to ML/AI systems

4. Legal and Regulatory Knowledge: Familiarity with data protection laws, AI regulations, and industry-specific compliance requirements

5. Technical Skills: Understanding of secure coding practices, cryptography, and security testing methodologies for ML/AI systems

6. Data Privacy: In-depth knowledge of data privacy principles and practices, particularly as they apply to ML/AI

7. Ethical AI: Understanding of ethical AI principles and experience in implementing responsible AI practices

8. Leadership: Strong leadership skills to guide teams and influence stakeholders across the organization

9. Communication: Excellent ability to communicate complex security concepts to both technical and non-technical audiences, including executive management

10. Strategic Thinking: Capacity to develop long-term security strategies that align with business objectives

11. Incident Response: Experience in managing security incidents and crisis situations

12. Continuous Learning: Commitment to staying updated on emerging ML/AI security threats and mitigation techniques

13. Project Management: Ability to manage complex, cross-functional security initiatives

14. Vendor Assessment: Skills in evaluating and managing security aspects of ML/AI vendors and tools

15. Financial Acumen: Understanding of the financial implications of security risks and the ability to justify security investments

This role requires a unique combination of technical expertise in both cybersecurity and ML/AI, along with strong leadership and strategic skills. The ML SecOps manager/director must be able to navigate the complex landscape of emerging technologies while managing the significant risks they pose to the enterprise.

Index

A

ACID, *see* Atomicity, Consistency, Isolation, Durability (ACID)

Adaptability, 18–20, 95, 100, 147

AI, *see* Artificial Intelligence (AI)

AI-driven decisions, 122, 123, 129, 131

AI-driven exponential growth, 123
- forecasting, 101
- organizational ambidexterity, 101
- shelf-life of skills, 101
- technological evolution, 101

AI Groupthink, 159, 160

AI Washing, 151–152

Annotation, 33, 178, 222

Apache Hadoop, 195, 219

Artificial Intelligence (AI), 123, 143, 152
- access controls, 41
- best practices in guidelines, 125, 126
- content creation, 66, 67
- credit card transactions, 62
- customer service, 67
- data hidden value, 75
- data management, 74, 75
- financial services, 68
- Gen AI models, 39
- governance, 39
- healthcare technology, 68, 69
- human resources, 68
- inventory and monitoring, 40
- policies, 123
- product design and development, 67
- production environment, 41
- recruitment, retention and promotion, 104
- revolution, 107–109
- risk assessments, 40
- security measures, 41
- training and awareness, 40

Asia, 121–122

Atomicity, Consistency, Isolation, Durability (ACID), 195

Automated machine learning (AutoML), 85, 86

Automated preprocessing, 33, 178

Automation, 16–17, 31, 57, 83, 84, 141–142, 152, 183–186, 244

A. J. O'Connor, *Organizing for Generative AI and the Productivity Revolution*, https://doi.org/10.1007/979-8-8688-0959-0